LOVE IN THE LITTLE THINGS

D0823929

LOVE
in the
LITTLE
THINGS

TALES OF FAMILY LIFE

MIKE AQUILINA

SERVANT
BOOKS

PUBLISHED BY FRANCISCAN MEDIA
Cincinnati, Ohio

Unless otherwise noted, Scripture passages have been taken from the *Revised Standard Version*, Catholic edition. Copyright ©1946, 1952, 1971 by the Division of Christian Education of the National Council of the Churches of Christ in the USA. Used by permission. All rights reserved.

(Note: The editors of this volume have made minor changes in capitalization to some of the Scripture quotations herein. Please consult the original source for proper capitalization.)

English translation of the *Catechism of the Catholic Church* for the United States of America Copyright ©1994, United States Catholic Conference, Inc.— Libreria Editrice Vaticana. English translation of the: *Catechism of the Catholic Church Modifications from the Editio Typica* Copyright ©1997, United States Catholic Conference, Inc.—Libreria Editrice Vaticana. Used with permission.

Cover design by Mark Sullivan
Cover photo ©www.istockphoto.com/Eric Isselée
Book design by Phillips Robinette, O.F.M.

LIBRARY OF CONGRESS CATALOGING-IN-PUBLICATION DATA

Aquilina, Mike.
  Love in the little things : tales of family life / Mike Aquilina.
      p. cm.
  ISBN 978-0-86716-814-3 (pbk. : alk. paper) 1. Family—Religious life. I. Title.

BX2351.A77 2007
248.4—dc22

                          2006037818

ISBN 978-0-86716-814-3
Copyright ©2007 Mike Aquilina. All rights reserved.

Published by Servant Books, an imprint of
Franciscan Media.
28 W. Liberty St.
Cincinnati, OH 45202
www.FranciscanMedia.org

Printed in the United States of America.

To Michael, my firstborn, who started
this project—in so many ways.

Contents

Foreword

Babies never doubt their need for a family; nor do small children. They live in utter dependency on their mom and dad and, to a lesser degree, their older siblings. Without help they can't eat or get dressed or hear their favorite stories read aloud. Without help they can't even reach the toys they want to play with.

Young children are on the receiving end of everything, and it makes for a good life. But at some point they become aware of yet another need: the need to be needed. They know that they're not quite in "full communion" with the older family members because they're not yet contributing their fair share. To be needed—and not just to be loved—is what it means to be fully engaged in family life.

One long-ago summer afternoon—I must have been very young, maybe five or six—I heard a scream from the kitchen. It was unmistakably Mom's voice. Immediately I bolted down the hall to see dear Mom backed up against—and half-sitting up on—the kitchen counter. I was really quite alarmed by her look of maternal terror. It was something I'd never seen before.

Her eyes were glued to the floor, and she could barely get the words out: "Th- th- there's a mouse!"

I remember the swirl of emotion. I kind of felt sorry for my mommy, seeing that nobody bigger than her youngest was around to deliver her from this plight. But as soon as my eyes caught sight of that threatening rodent (it was actually quite tiny, almost cute), the realization dawned that my mother needed me—little me.

With the fire of filial courage suddenly inflaming my little-boy breast, off I went after that pesky mouse. After cornering it, I grabbed it by the tail and picked it up. It was so very small, teeny-tiny. But it was apparent that its size made no difference to Mom, since that same terror was still in her eyes.

I then asked what seemed to be a very logical question: "What should I do?"

"Just get it out of here!"

Dutifully I walked out of the kitchen, a short way down the hall and into the bathroom, where I spied the toilet. What better fate to befall any creature that would terrorize my mom? With a splash and a flush, it was over.

My entire heroic action had taken less than a minute, but I knew that I had ascended to a new plane of human existence. For the first time in my life, *Mom needed me!* I actually could meet the needs of the person who had been meeting all of mine, all my life. It was a moment of illumination, a full initiation into family life, a first glimpse of a mystery that dwelt at the heart of our home.

What I glimpsed was the mysterious and inseparable relationship between love and sacrifice. We need to be needed for our own unique contribution, our own unique gifts. What we have been given we long to give away in turn, and we won't be happy until we fulfill that longing, until we give ourselves to someone else in love, holding nothing back.

The family is where these needs are satisfied in the natural way that God ordained. In his autobiography Saint Augustine spoke of the family as a network of mutual, natural needs, which are really God's gentle way of getting us to love one another.[1] The sacrament of marriage raises these natural drives and natural fulfillment to a supernatural level, so that all our loving and all our giving prepare us for the supreme and ultimate act of loving and giving, which we call heaven.

My friend Mike Aquilina often speaks of the family in terms of love and sacrifice. *Love and sacrifice:* These elements combine in a combustible way in the pages of this book. The mystery burns at this book's heart, as it burns in Mike's own heart. I should know. I work with Mike, so I know him as a provider who looks out for his family. And Mike and I have been friends since we were both young dads, so I can attest that these essays are true, even at their silliest—especially at their silliest.

I'm pleased to say that I was there when Mike first laughed about these lessons of family life. I'm pleased now to see them in print, for the benefit of many more families.

Scott Hahn
Professor of Theology and Scripture
Franciscan University of Steubenville

Acknowledgments

If this were the kind of book that piled footnotes into the bottom margins of its pages, you'd see the names of my parents and my wife's parents all over the place. So much of what Terri and I know about love we learned from them: Mike and Mary Aquilina and Glenn and Ruth Shupp.

My brothers and sisters come next. Since I'm the youngest of seven, and since I am nine years younger than the next-youngest sib, those six were like a flock of extra parents, always doting on me. They are, in birth order, Florence (Duffy), Susie (Sullivan), Mary (Hanczyc), Rosaria (Baldino), Charlie and Joe.

But it's really my wife and kids who made this book possible. They've made the living of this life so much fun that I couldn't resist telling the story. Terri and I are the proud parents of Michael Joseph, Mary Agnes, Rosemary Louise, Grace Marie, Isabella Maria and Teresa Carmella.

Finally, I have to thank my friends who have been victims of my compulsive storytelling. These guys have, for years, endured my inability to tell a funny story without dissolving into laughter myself. It usually takes me several tries to get to the punch line, and by then only the most patient can still follow the thread. (This is one reason why I write for a living.)

Those who suffer most are my coworkers at the St. Paul Center: Scott Hahn, David Scott and Rob Corzine. My friends Jack Nelson, Brian Donnelly and David Mills have also sat through countless dress rehearsals of these chapters. I tip my hat to you, one and all.

Some of these essays began as columns for various publications through the ages, especially *New Covenant*, which I edited from 1996 to 2002; the *Pittsburgh Catholic*, which I edited from 1993 to 1996; *Our Sunday Visitor* and *Lay Witness*. I thank the editors and publishers of these publications for giving me good guidance, good pay and firm deadlines. The essays I wrote for their pages have been radically revised for this book; so please, gentle reader, don't blame my former publishers for what you find here!

If you like what you read here, however, you should thank Cynthia Cavnar of Servant Books, who helped to shape a manuscript out of a few conversations. Cindy is an actual grace.

Finally, I wish to thank a twentieth-century churchman, Saint Josemaría Escrivá, whose writings have influenced me, especially in my thinking about marriage and family. For me it all comes down to nitty-gritty advice like this:

People who are constantly concerned with themselves, who act above all for their own satisfaction, endanger their eternal salvation and cannot avoid being unhappy even in this life. Only if a person forgets himself and gives himself to God and to others, in marriage as well as in any other aspect of life, can he be happy on this earth, with a happiness that is a preparation for, and a foretaste of, the joy of heaven.[1]

Introduction: Love Amid the Frostbite

The poet W.H. Auden once said that you can learn everything you need to know about an editor if you ask him to tell you his idea of Eden, of earthly paradise. Since I'm an editor by trade, my answer to that question should serve as a good introduction to this book. Know my paradise, and you'll know what I wish for my family. You'll know the ideal for which I'm striving.

Now, if I were just out to score brownie points, I'd answer Mr. Auden's question simply, as one editor did—"Paradise? My wife!"—and then get on with the stories that make up the heart of the book. But brownie points rank only around second on my list of priorities. For when you and I consider the Catholic notion of family life, we're acknowledging the presence of an even higher authority than my wife, Terri.

The Bible, of course, sets a good model for any Christian who would describe paradise. Believers don't just look ahead to a time when life will be pleasant and humans will do what they're supposed to do. We begin by looking back on such a time. So I'd like to introduce myself by telling you the story of the most improbably paradisal day of my life.

Pennsylvania winters can be brutal, and nowhere so brutal as at the university in the geographic center of the state, the place that young residents ironically call "Happy Valley." Penn

State University sprawls over many square miles in a valley that serves as a natural wind tunnel. On a spring day students can build muscles by pushing against a stiff wind as they rush from class to class. But there are no such silver linings to the gray storm cloud of a Penn State winter. Wind means one thing and one thing only: the wind-chill factor. It means leaning into strong, bitter gusts in a good mile trek from one corner of campus to another.

Now magnify all those conditions by a nineteen-year-old guy's capacity for self-pity, and you see that the suffering of such a winter could be immense and even desperate. ("Mom, please send more money for pizza delivery. Frostbite stands between me and the dining hall.")

Well, it was in the dead of such a winter that I met Her, the occasion of my nearest brush with idolatry. She was Terri Shupp, a little wisp of a girl from Gettysburg whose smile could melt the campus's highest snowbank and whose intelligence and wit made for sparkling conversation that I wanted never, ever to end.

I was even willing to rise at dawn to start the conversation, if only she would let me. One below-zero Saturday morning she didn't have time to spend with me, because she was volunteering for some do-good cause way across campus.

"I'll walk you over," I broke in. "I can be there in a minute."

It probably took no more than half a minute for me to be fully suited for the weather, transported across the street and sitting in the lobby of Terri's dorm. She arrived radiant but a little late, and after quick greetings, she led the way to the door. I followed, dazzled, outside.

I didn't care at all about the cold, nor did I care that her volunteer gig was on the other side of creation. The farther away the better. We could talk the whole way. She could make me laugh. Maybe I could make her laugh too. This was living.

We had gone maybe a quarter of a mile when I noticed that she was rubbing her bare hands together before returning them to her pockets. In her rush to get downstairs, she had forgotten to wear gloves. Her hands must have been in pain already.

I didn't have to think twice. "Gosh, you're going to get frostbite. Take my gloves."

She protested, but I insisted. And she put them on.

Soon my hands had no feeling. I loved it. After a little bit more time they were turning strange colors. This walk was costing a fortune in terms of human endurance, but I was willing to pay the price. The more my hands ached, the more I felt I was loving her. I was *proving* my love. Like the knights of the Middle Ages, I was taking on an ordeal for the love of My Lady, and I was prevailing, without a word of complaint and with a constant smile.

By the time I said good-bye and Terri sprinted into the building to do her hours of good for the world, I was fairly well pointed in the direction of matrimony, with or without my hands, which seemed as if they might require amputation. It didn't matter. If I had fallen dead from frostbite, to have my flesh consumed by arctic wolves and mountain lions, I could not have died happier.

To think that a gloveless walk in icy wind—a situation I would have bemoaned on the way to a first-period psychology class—could be nothing less than paradise on this particular morning. The sacrifice itself was glorious. But as I was to learn, love moves from glory to greater glory.

Evening came, and morning followed, and who should appear very early at my door but Terri Shupp. She had stopped by to return my gloves. I kept her there as long as I could, and when she left I actually put my unworthy hands in one of the gloves she had worn on her most lovely hands. Then and there I learned that virtuous acts do receive their just reward. She had left a note for me in each finger of both gloves.

Fast-forward many years, beyond our marriage in 1985, beyond the birth of our first four children in 1989, 1992, 1994 and 1997, to the year 2000, when Terri and I were invited to give a talk to engaged couples. We spoke on the subject of love and sacrifice, and I built my talk around the story of that winter day when we were very young. Terri applied the underlying principles to many aspects of marital life. Our bottom line was that people are happier when they're living to make others happy.

One man raised his hand and addressed his question to me: "If you're always living to make her happy, when do you ever get to have fun?"

I was struck dumb by the question. I must have just stared at the guy, because the priest running the program spoke up and gave the right answer.

I suppose I'm not good at theoretical answers anyway. I like to tell stories, and I like to read stories. And that's what this book is all about.

If there is a recurring theme in the book, it is the point that Terri and I tried to make to those engaged couples: happiness requires love, and love requires sacrifice. For me this is the summary of all Catholic teaching—on family life, on sexual morality, on social justice, not to mention the Trinity, the Incarnation and the Eucharist.

The family is the great catechism God has given the world. The work of our lifetime is to learn how to read it and then study it prayerfully.

A couple in love will learn many lessons in the everyday events of their life together. Throw into the mix a child or two (or six or twelve), and the lessons increase by orders of magnitude. It's all serious business, I suppose, but a sense of humor plays no small part in our spiritual development.

Monks may learn humility by wearing a hair shirt; we parents have our own means of mortification. We must, for example, sit helpless while our four-year-old daughter, patiently and with scientific rigor, enlightens a visiting elderly, saintly Franciscan priest about the varieties of panties that Mattel affixes to its Barbie dolls. (I'm not making this up.)

We must decrease as our spouses increase in importance. We must decrease as our children increase in wisdom, age and strength. And the first thing to go is any puffed-up sense of our own dignity. (I mean, Barbie panties, really!)

Yet we need not be diminished at the core. Pope John Paul II often urged young couples to "become what you are" by giving themselves away.[1] This is something we'd never do voluntarily, but it's something that parenting forces upon us. Parenting is God's way of making Christianity simpler for people like me, who by nature are not too quick on the uptake.

How simple is it? Saint Paul put it plainly for Christian spouses and parents: "I appeal to you … by the mercies of God, to present your bodies as a living sacrifice, holy and acceptable to God, which is your spiritual worship" (Romans 12:1). In this book I present that living sacrifice in living color, with stories of how I've grown with my kids, from diapers through puberty. I hope readers will learn with me, and I hope they'll laugh with me.

Our family life is the sacrifice we offer to God every day. It rises like incense to heaven as we do very ordinary things: as we love our spouses, guide our kids, pay the bills, attend countless, endless scout meetings and do our work. All this is our share in the common priesthood of the church. It is our daily sacrifice, the Mass we live.

God, for his part, gives back to us abundantly, from the treasury of his own perfect fatherhood. His grace empowers us to reach it all—eternal happiness, lasting love and loving sacrifice. And that's the only way we can find fulfillment and become who we are as parents.

As we lift up our hearts in this sacrifice, God stoops down to lift up our homes, to make them outposts of his paradise, havens of charity and happiness, no matter how cold the winds may blow on a winter day.

ONE

Our Daring, Real-Life Adventures

The two treasure hunters whispered in the darkness of the forest. By the light of a match, they peered over the map they had taken—in a fair fight, of course—from the wicked pirates. Getting up, they quietly made their way to the three stones at the foot of the mountain. They tapped their walking stick three times on the large middle stone. In a flash a cave yawned open before them..."

One fateful evening when my son was three—an evening when he was desperate for distraction—I told him a story about the two of us. We were on a boat on the Monongahela River, in search of a Spanish galleon that had been sunk four hundred years before near Pittsburgh, just a few miles from our home. (Note to critics: Desperate needs for distraction allow one to contradict the facts of geography and history and the laws of physics.) Michael and I sent divers down to the wreck, and we found the rotting hull, filled of course with oaken chests overflowing with gold, silver, diamonds, sapphires, emeralds, rubies and pearls.

The story kept Michael amused as long as it had to. But it worked too well. After a year I was still telling it—every night.

"Put a ghost into it, Daddy, and some knights and lots of danger," my son would say.

So I did. And together Michael and I wound our way through dark mountain forests, set sail across even darker seas and searched through haunted castles for hidden trapdoors. All the while a combined and ominous force of pirates and ghosts pursued us.

What is it that made these stories so thrilling to a three-year-old?

G.K. Chesterton once wrote that baptism begins the greatest adventure there is. In faith we struggle constantly to serve a Love we cannot prove. We struggle daily against dark supernatural forces that wish our demise. Awesome supernatural forces of light assist us: the angels of heaven. And we travel our road with a rough and merry band, some living and others dead (but still with us nonetheless), the communion of saints.

If we see our life at home and our days at work with eyes of faith, we find ourselves in the midst of a story that makes Michael's wildest tales look tame.

How much mightier than magic are the sacraments, those channels of grace from the very God who made the angels, the planets, the volcanoes and the dinosaurs? How much more perilous than shark-infested seas is a near occasion of sin? How much more powerful than a *Star Trek* communicator is the simplest of our prayers?

What author would demand such a willing suspension of disbelief as we all make every Sunday when we recite the outlandish Nicene Creed—life everlasting, indeed!—and we consume eternity in hardly a mouthful at Holy Communion?

The adventure Michael desires is nothing more than the life he already has, the life he gained on his baptismal day. He hungers for the faith to live it to the full, to see things as they are.

And who doesn't? Look at the time and money that grown-ups lavish on fantasy TV, games and books—*Dungeons and Dragons, Harry Potter, Star Wars*—and virtual reality. Who needs it? There's enough adventure in *real* reality—the bus ride into the city, the trip to the grocery store, the dinner on the stove.

"With their crowbar they jimmied open the lid of the chest. Treasures sparkled before them in the lantern light: tens of thousands of gold doubloons."

"And bubble gum, Daddy, and pizza?"

"And bubble gum and pizza."

Two

Mom and Pop and Property Rights

A few times a day I hear myself tell my toddler daughter, "Put that down. That's Daddy's." And she puts it down—the memento or the fragile bauble or the prized book.

I have to wonder where I learned the words "That's Daddy's." They're not in my first language, the one I learned from Mom and Pop. I mimicked my parents' pleases and thank-yous, hellos and good-byes. But I can't recall a time when they taught me "mine"—at least not by example.

When I was growing up, my parents lived a life of renunciation that now seems almost Franciscan. They renounced their time, calling none of it their own. My father worked long, very hard hours for a coal company. When he came home exhausted, I'll bet he wanted nothing more than to collapse beneath the newspaper, but he collapsed beneath kids instead. He would wrestle with me on the floor, let me crawl on him, pounce on him—let me live the dream of any child who's read Dr. Seuss's *Hop on Pop*. Eventually he'd drift off to sleep, while my game went on with him as a prop.

My parents renounced their possessions too. I can remember every detail of the small metal box that held our family's insurance policies and birth certificates. I remember it because it was the only thing in the house that was off-limits. We had open season on everything else. My mother's rosary, necklaces, brooches and bracelets filled a small pirate's cardboard chest to overflowing. (Where *did* I bury it?) And she never said, "Put that down."

Mom and Pop renounced privacy. We kids grumbled because we had none: six of us filled (and I do mean filled) two beds in two small rooms (and I do mean small). But my parents had no room of their own. Their bed filled an opening, a dent really, in the hallway.

My mother renounced her peeves too. She's orderly by nature. But if I close my eyes, I still can conjure up the disorder I imposed on every available inch of our floor—toys, sneakers, books, crayons, papers...

They renounced their interests. If they ever wanted to do anything but play with us kids, I never noticed. Even with my own kids, I never saw Pop converse with one eye on the TV. My mother has never worried about her own plate while filling mine with pasta, chicken, meatballs, Italian sausage, homemade bread...

I can recall only one lesson on property from my childhood. Once, when I had scrawled on one of my father's books, he told me, "Our books are our friends." I still find it hard to take notes in books.

But somehow, somewhere, I forgot the really valuable lessons of my childhood. Instead I learned to hoard property, call it my own, shelve trinkets high out of the reach of little hands. And I learned to nurse my peeves and interests and pleasures.

I'm the youngest of the children of Mike and Mary Aquilina. Maybe my older sisters and brothers can remember a time when my parents had a speck more of the selfishness that's "normal" in parents. I can't.

The great Pope Paul VI knew instinctively when he wrote his encyclical *Humanae Vitae* that childrearing is a refiner's fire. The demands, the work and the love burn away the self, the self, the self.

By the time Mom and Pop got around to having me, maybe they'd been rendered, quite literally, selfless. Emptied of self, they could be filled with Christ. At least it seems that way to me.

THREE

It's Verse Than I Imagined

My soulful poet, my brown-eyed bard, is Mary Agnes, my second-born. We first discovered her talents when she was three and one night recited an original composition to her cousin Mark:

Somewhere along my joyful feet,
my eyes are in a carrot pool.

Terri and I concluded that the French surrealists must have influenced Mary Agnes. This phase of her poetic achievement continued for quite some time, producing at least one other masterpiece, which began:

The watermelons are all in the station,
singing to the blackbirds in the rain.

OK, so I'm as prone as any parent to exaggerate the talents of my children. But I've studied prosody enough to recognize that Mary Agnes has a good sense of meter. So I decided to encourage her interest as best I could. I took to reading her some simple but great poems before bed at night: selections from William Blake's *Songs of Innocence* and some of Theodore Roethke's nonsense verse and animal poems. She seemed to enjoy it, if only because it involved concentrated attention from a doting dad.

When Mary Agnes was five, I typed up all our favorites in a little chapbook and gave it to her for Christmas. The following year, when we moved, I noticed that she packed the little book among her favorite things.

As she grew in wisdom, age and grace—turning seven—Mary Agnes would blush a deep red whenever her brother recited her old surrealist masterworks. He, of course, tuned in to this immediately and proposed a recital whenever two or more were gathered and one of them happened to be his sister. Probably because of this unsought literary limelight, Mary Agnes began to keep quiet about whatever the muses might be whispering to her. But her ordinary speech continued to show a keen sense of rhythm and sound.

One day when she was still six, she rushed into my office, crying softly because a small playmate had driven a toy car over her favorite doll, leaving a long crack from its forehead to the base of its neck. Mary Agnes said she felt as if it had happened to her. "I felt my own heart break," she sobbed.

Inconsolable, she wept on my leg, as her brother—100 percent male—tried to reason with her grief. "It's just a doll. We can get another. Or we can get it repaired. Look"—he produced a hefty volume of the Yellow Pages—"there are four listings under 'Doll Repair'!"

He was doing his best. But even if he had had a clue about grief, consolation or the sensitivities of poets, he couldn't have done any good. Mary Agnes needed to cry.

And I needed to pray that God would call all my children to monastic enclosure before they encountered any real trials—trials that I couldn't bear. For when Mary Agnes felt her doll's heart break, I felt my own heart break, and my favorite poets raised forebodings in my mind:

Ah! as the heart grows older
It will come to such sights colder
By and by, nor spare a sigh...
And yet you will weep and know why.[1]

Alas, my small surrealist was entering her realist phase. In the long run it makes for poetry that's more to my taste. Yet it means too that I must begin the long, long struggle to give my Mary Agnes more completely to a better Father, a Father who will always be there when she weeps and knows why, a Father who heals broken hearts—while I stand helpless to fix a little doll.

Four

Pilgrim's Progress

Old St. Patrick's is a hidden treasure in the city of Pittsburgh. Ringed by stone walls like a monastery, the church hides amid long rows of warehouses and meat packers. Its street side faces a rail yard. More than once I've seen a rat scuttle by as I ducked in for a visit.

But inside its walls are paradisal beauties: a sculpture garden, hung all around with diamonds of ice in winter, brilliant with emerald life in spring.

Not two centuries ago Saint John Neumann was pastor in St. Pat's neighborhood. He shared a rectory there with Blessed Francis X. Seelos. Both were Redemptorist priests. Father John, later to be bishop of Philadelphia, was known hereabouts for his cheer and his charity. Only after his death would his flock learn of the severe penances he practiced, all the while he smiled upon his people and loved them so well.

Such heroic penance seems a legacy of St. Pat's. A later pastor installed what stands today as the church's centerpiece, the *sacra scala* or "holy stairs." A sign at the entrance forbids anyone to set foot on the marble stairs; we may only ascend on our knees. From the bottom it's almost impossible to see the goal. But faith knows: The *sacra scala* ends at the foot of the church's tabernacle.

I make a pilgrimage there whenever I can. Once I took my kindergarten-aged son to St. Pat's, and he eagerly accepted the challenge of the stairs, racing up once on his knees, offering his prayer, coming down, then racing up again. Ah, to be six again. He was praying, he said, for someone's conversion.

I know whose. She's a dear friend of ours. Once I took her, too, to St. Pat's, and she—a conventional Protestant—described her experience in almost mystical terms. It was an emerald green day, and she knew the presence of Jesus Christ.

Oscar Wilde wrote, "Where there is sorrow, there is holy ground,"[1] and I'm willing to believe it. The graces we reap casually today were sown by the penances of generations long before us—butchers and rail workers and washerwomen taking one painful step after another. "We are afflicted in every way, . . . always carrying in the body the death of Jesus, so that the life of Jesus may also be manifested in our bodies. . . . So death is at work in us, but life in you" (2 Corinthians 4:8, 10, 12).

We each take our turn, like Saint John Neumann and Saint Paul, making up in our own flesh what is lacking in the suffering of Christ for the sake of his body, the church (see Colossians 1:24). We pray sacrificially, we fast, we make pilgrimages, and we give alms penitentially—that is, till it hurts. Because then it heals, not only ourselves but also others.

The spirit of penance and mortification is a healing ministry in the body of Christ, and it isn't optional. The Master tells us that unless we deny ourselves and take up his cross daily, we cannot be his disciples (see Matthew 10:38). The church, his people, needs our sacrifices.

And we needn't knit a hair shirt in order to do our part. An ordinary parent's ordinary day is covered with more rough spots than any coarse woolen garment. Right now, for example, my oldest child—who knows that I'm on deadline—is interrupting me with at least his fortieth question of the day. Each time I turn to answer him, I take another step. Each time my wife wipes up another grape-juice spill or issues a reminder for Mary Agnes to clean her room, there's yet another rung on the ladder that leads to heaven.

We can make each sacrifice silently, with a smile, as Saint John Neumann did, and we should offer each for a purpose, an intention: that this child might overcome his toxic temper, that the other child might be less lazy, that my siblings will return to the sacraments, that my ancestors may gain release from purgatory, that my far-off descendants will keep the faith.

The holy stairs are arduous. But for the price of a moment's discomfort, we find ourselves at the throne of glory, where every prayer is heard.

We needn't fly to Rome or Jerusalem to make a pilgrimage. Old St. Pat's is one of our family's favorites, and it's just a twenty-five-minute drive on a weekend. What treasures are hidden in the history of your local church, your communion of saints?

FIVE

Bread of Laugh

We never argued about religion, the beautiful Lutheran woman and I. We did have many discussions, especially in the first two years of marriage. Once she asked me to explain the difference between Lutheran and Catholic doctrines on the Eucharist.

Eruditely I dug up a copy of *Luther's Small Catechism* and paced the floor as I quoted that, according to her church, the sacrament "is the true body and blood of our Lord Jesus Christ, under the bread and wine, instituted by Christ himself for us Christians to eat and to drink."[1] Then I pulled down my old *Baltimore Catechism* and read: "After the substance of the bread and wine had been changed into the substance of the body and blood of Our Lord, there remained only the appearances of bread and wine."[2]

"Catholics believe," I explained, "that the real presence means Jesus is there—body, blood, soul and divinity—even after Mass, when the sacrament is reserved in the tabernacle. And there's no longer a crumb we can call bread or a drop we can call wine."

Then that beautiful woman looked up at me from her chair and laughed.

My eyebrows went up. "What's so funny?"

"You don't believe that," she said.

"Yes, I do."

"No, you don't," she replied. "If you do, then why do you only go to Mass on Sunday? You don't even visit the church during the week."

Since that conversation in 1986, I've been to Mass just about every day, and I try not to pass the church without stopping in for a visit to the tabernacle. By her laughter Terri brought home a powerful truth. Not that Catholics have to go to Mass every day; we don't. But why didn't I want to? Why had it never occurred to me that I might go to Communion more often than just Sunday? It took the laughter of God's messenger to change me.

I think of that incident every year as the Feast of Corpus Christi approaches. More formally called the "Solemnity of the Body and Blood of Christ," it's the day when the church celebrates Jesus' abiding presence in the Eucharist. Because of my experience I've declared this feast my personal holiday to thank the Lord for the good fruits of ecumenical dialogue and to pray for the day when all Christians are reunited as a family around one common table.

Our Lord himself prayed for Christian unity, so we can be sure that it will happen. Of course, there's plenty of nastiness we have to get over first, and there are doctrinal differences that cannot be resolved short of conversion. But the Good Shepherd is doing the gathering, and he can work miracles.

Since 1991 my own family has lived the beautiful communion that I wish for the whole church. That year I witnessed the miracle I had long stopped dreaming of. At the Easter Vigil Terri was received into the Roman Catholic Church.

So there's much I can be thankful for on Corpus Christi. What we can't seem to accomplish in ecclesiastical boardrooms and windy documents—or arguments, disputes and demonstrations—maybe we can achieve with a song, a prayer and the well-timed laughter of a loved one in the Lord.

SIX

Mama Said

Mama said there'd be days like this.

You know the days I'm talking about. You've shelled out a significant portion of your income for a major appliance. It's delivered to your door, and it doesn't work. Then you spend a week or so on the phone trying, unsuccessfully, to talk to the folks who were only too eager to take your call before they cashed your check.

My mother has a way of dealing with these problems when they come her children's way. The source of our troubles, she surmises, is malnutrition. (You've heard about the famine in Pittsburgh?) So she cooks for us—delights from millennia of Sicilian tradition, in quantities larger than a regiment would need.

Mom knows how to console her seven children, now all grown and flown from the nest. But consolation isn't everything we need, and she knows that too, so it's hardly all she dispenses. I know, for example, that she would probably take me to task for the way I'm fuming at the helpless customer service representative on the other end of the phone and for the way I'm fuming about his employer when I slam down the receiver. As a matter of fact, my mother would have something to say about the way I slam down the receiver.

The late great Catholic physician Herbert Ratner meditated deeply on how God makes mothers for loving. "The focal length of the newborn's vision," he once wrote, "...is about nine inches, a measure that approximates the distance from the baby at the breast to the mother's eyes and face." The female voice is pitched high to match precisely the sensitivity of a newborn's hearing.[1]

Theologian Father William Virtue, a disciple of Dr. Ratner, refers to motherhood as "a lay priesthood." The mother, he says, is the first to mediate God's goodness to the child.[2] Our mothers' milk, smiles and lullabies are our first intimations of God's providence and his love.

Saint Augustine wrote that the deepest human desire is to look upon one who looks back in love.[3] This is the gift God gives us from the beginning, but little by little, in increments and in longing. The gift will be fulfilled perfectly in heaven.

Anyone who has known a mother's love can come to see why our heavenly Father gave us all a common mother in the Blessed Virgin Mary. The truth of Mary's love for me was among the earliest lessons I learned from my mom. While I was an infant at the breast, I'm sure, I learned the cadence of the rosary. In time I would sort out the words of the Hail Mary, the Memorare, the Angelus, the Hail, Holy Queen.

And my mother has always lived by the words she prayed with us and taught us. Today, when I see a Marian image, it fades into the image of my mom. In spending so much time together, Mary and Mom have begun to look alike.

"Whoever does not receive the kingdom of God like a child," our Savior tells us, "shall not enter it" (Mark 10:15). We need to recognize once again our helplessness amid the contradictions of life—the failed appliances and whatnot—and we need to relearn the precious limits we had as babies: to look upward to find peace and to see no further than our mother's face.

SEVEN

A Universal Call to Party

My kids seem to love the Catholic faith. And why not? The church packs the calendar with dozens of reasons to party. To our family's way of thinking, "practicing Catholics" are those who celebrate the most.

Like when? On feast days of our patron saints, the major solemnities of the church, holy days of obligation, Marian feasts.... We'll seize any excuse to bake something chocolate or drive to a favorite inexpensive restaurant.

Several years back Pope John Paul II issued another call to festivities: "We should celebrate the day of our baptism as we do our birthday!" he exclaimed one year on January 12, the Feast of the Baptism of the Lord.[1]

Now, there's nothing our family would like more than to add another party to our calendar. But this one was already on. Since October 14, 1990, the first anniversary of my oldest child's baptism, we've marked all our children's baptismal days with a special dinner and dessert—and a little remembrance.

It only makes sense: if birth is so important that it marks a major touchstone every year, shouldn't our *rebirth* in Christ be even more important? Birth gave us natural life, which is great, but baptism gave us eternal life, which is greatness itself.

What did the pope mean when he asked us to celebrate? Well, celebrations are meant to be fun. So maybe baptism day isn't the day to read the *Catechism of the Catholic Church*'s section on the sacraments aloud, in its entirety, to our assembled children. But we do recall, at least briefly, what the day is all about: when we can we invite the godparents over for dinner. Then, after dinner but before the cake, we follow a little ritual.

First we light the child's baptismal candle. Then, with the candle lit, we read one of the Scripture passages relating to the sacrament. There are many good ones to choose from. Our favorites are Matthew 19:13-15 ("Let the children come to me..."), John 3:5 (on being "born of water and the Spirit") and Mark 1:9-11 (on Jesus' own baptism).

After the reading all of us renew our baptismal promises. (You can find the promises in many popular prayer books and also in the Easter Vigil liturgy in a missalette—ask your parish priest for a copy of an old one.) We conclude with an Our Father, blow out the candle, then dig into dessert.

Before you conclude that our family is "different" and that this wouldn't work in your home, let me emphasize the fact that the goings-on don't approach the majesty of a high Mass at the cathedral. In fact, they're more like panels from Bil Keane's *Family Circus* comic strip.

Amid the solemnities our two-year-old inevitably tries to blow out the candle. Our seven-year-old mispronounces a good bit of what she reads. Our four-year-old feels compelled to interrupt the Gospel reading with her narrative of a baptism she once attended in New Jersey, where the baby wouldn't stop crying and the godparents were late and.... You get the idea. It's all part of the fun, and celebrations *should* be fun.

In his 1994 apostolic exhortation *Tertio Millennio Adveniente* ("On the Coming Third Millennium"), Pope John

Paul II issued his call to "a renewed appreciation of Baptism as the basis of Christian living." [2]

"We should celebrate the day of our baptism as we do our birthday!" he told us in 1997. But then he added, "How many of the baptized are fully aware of what they have received? We must give a new impetus to catechesis, to rediscover this gift which also means taking on a great responsibility." [3]

And it all begins, like most good things, in the home. Religion doesn't have to be dull or dreary or burdensome. The Catholic faith sometimes can be as fun, as crazy and as memorable as a family birthday celebration.

So, anyone up for a party?

EIGHT

Loving Hearts and Replacement Parts

The ancients put a lot of stock in the human heart. Search the Scriptures, and you'll find the heart described as the seat of the intellect, the conscience, the emotions, the passions and the will. It's a lot of work, but some organ had to do it.

Besides, the sages usually assigned the complex workings of romantic love to the liver. That division of labor kept the heart free, no doubt, to worry over such urgent matters as wisdom, heaven and geometry.

Nowadays, of course, we know that the heart is merely a muscle that pumps blood to keep the machine running. When the pump slows, leaks or flutters, we can call in a surgeon to tune it up. Many of my close friends—and now my father-in-law, too—have endured such a tune-up in the last few years. I know the procedure by now: the doctors take a length of artery from the leg, then break the patient's ribs and fit the leg artery portion as a bypass for the heart's clogged plumbing.

All of this cracking and tearing hurts a body for some time afterward. My father-in-law wondered aloud if he would always feel as lousy as he felt the week after his surgery—and if so, how was it worth the trouble?

But the pain does seem to bring about a gain. A few months later Grandpa—trim, exercised and full of vigor—said he hadn't felt so good since he was a teenager. In his case and many others of which I've known, the patients—men and women of ample wisdom going into surgery—seem to have grown wiser through the ordeal. So maybe the ancients were on to something after all.

The suffering of heart surgery is remedial, something people endure so that they can continue to enjoy life. They consent to the surgery only when they're convinced of a threat to the heart, sometimes a threat that's discernible only to the most sensitive of medical gadgetry.

Far more painful than cardiac rehab is the suffering of a broken heart (according to the modern literary sense of the organ). In the midst of family quarrels, sibling rivalries and generational differences, we wonder indeed whether we'll feel this way the rest of our lives and why God allows us to suffer.

Yet this suffering, too, should be remedial. The lesson of the crucifix is that even the cruelest and most humiliating heartbreak can save not only one's own soul but the world as well. For those who suffer with Christ are not content to be mere victims of a sacrifice but priests as well. They actively make the offering of their lives, and they begin by getting their interior lives in order. Suffering has led many a soul to self-knowledge, which in turn leads to penance, which is the one remedy we all need.

Then true healing has begun, from the inside out. "A broken and contrite heart, O God, you will not despise" (Psalm 51:17).

NINE

Say That Again

Some decades ago I lived in a parish that was just beginning a new program for Sunday visits to sick parishioners. Since I lived a block away from the rectory and Terri and I had no children at the time, I got "volunteered" for just about everything, and this program was no exception.

It was no great trouble, really. I was probably the parishioner best equipped to handle Pennsylvania weather. I drove a tank of a car, a powder blue 1970 Dodge Coronet with a 440 engine. Winter could do little to hinder me as I rolled along the back roads. Nor need I hesitate at the nearly vertical hills I encountered en route to the hospital.

I learned, however, to be open to surprises of a different order.

Once I visited the hospital room of a man who had suffered a stroke. He was an usher in our parish, so I knew him in passing. He apologized for not remembering me, but after the stroke, he explained, he didn't remember anyone, including his wife, his son and his daughter. Still, he could speak and listen with little difficulty. His family, he said, was slowly reintroducing him through photos from his years of marriage.

I had the task of reintroducing him to Jesus Christ. And I have to confess, I didn't feel up to it. It had been a long day; his room was my last stop; I was exhausted.

I began by reading him the gospel of the day. I don't remember the passage, but it was one that you and I have heard a thousand times in our adult lives. I was reciting it for the umpteenth time that day, and I was probably thinking about going home to my wife and my dinner.

Abruptly the man stopped me by placing his hand on my book. "Wait a minute," he said. "Say that again."

I repeated the phrase I had just read.

"That's amazing," he said. "That's amazing." I saw he had tears in his eyes. It struck me then that this man was hearing the gospel for the first time. And he was bowled over by its good news.

On my drive home I asked our Lord to restore the newness of the gospel to my heart and mind. What that man gained from circumstance I wanted to have by grace.

That's been my prayer ever since, through many changes in my life. Having children only confirmed the need for me. If we want our sons and daughters to sense the excitement of faith, if we want them to know the adventure at the heart of all great literature, if we want them to experience wonder at the intricacies of creation as they pursue their studies in the sciences, if we want them to feel the joy of friendship with Jesus, then we have to communicate the *newness* of life in Christ, even many years after our baptism or conversion. We have to radiate the newness of the gospel even decades after we have heard it for the hundredth time.

Paradoxically, we sustain our love by growing older in close company with the object of our love. This is true of marriage, and it's true of our life of faith. We need to spend time in the company of our beloved, in conversation and in the quiet too. No matter what the old proverbs say, no heart will grow fonder through absence from Jesus Christ.

We mustn't wait for a medical condition to restore the new-ness of love to our spiritual life. We may not get the particular grace that that old man received in his hospital room. And the gospel is eternal anyway, so it never grows old. But we have to cultivate its newness in our own lives through sustained and disciplined prayer and study.

God will give us the grace, but what we do with it is our business. He leaves us free to accept or reject his love, and we make that choice every day, building on the choice we made the day before.

Moments of illumination arrive maybe once in a thousand hospital visits. But our growth in love is a matter of the will's corresponding to God's grace, exercised day after day after day after day.

TEN

Your Priesthood

D o you think your son will be a priest?"

My son Michael, now a teenager, is a good kid, and often enough we hear the question. If God wants Michael to be ordained, I pray that he'll respond faithfully. But even if God calls him another way—say, to marriage—I hope Michael grows up with a full appreciation of his holy priesthood.

"You are a chosen race, a royal priesthood," wrote Saint Peter, the first pope, to the churches of the East (1 Peter 2:9). He was not writing merely to his clergy but to people like you and me. Pope John Paul II echoed those words in his 1988 Apostolic Exhortation on the Laity, *Christifideles Laici*.

The priesthood of the laity "has never been forgotten in the living tradition of the Church," the Holy Father wrote.[1] True, but we Catholics have treaded cautiously in this area since Martin Luther's distortions of four centuries ago. Luther claimed the priesthood of all believers as a justification for dismantling the sacramental priesthood.

But it's not. The priesthood of the laity is a necessary complement to the priesthood of the clergy. When someone asked Cardinal Newman why laypeople should matter, he replied that the clergy would look pretty silly without them.

If we're to understand our priesthood, we first have to ask, what is a priest? A quick answer is that a priest is one who offers sacrifice. Indeed, Saint Peter's letter directs its readers "to be a holy priesthood, to offer spiritual sacrifices acceptable to God through Jesus Christ" (1 Peter 2:5).

We know when our parish priest offers his principal sacrifice: in the Mass. But when do we offer ours?

"Incorporated in Jesus Christ," said Pope John Paul II, "the baptized are united to him and to his sacrifice in the offering they make of themselves and their daily activities.... 'For their work, prayers and apostolic endeavors, their ordinary married and family life, their daily labor, their mental and physical relaxation, if carried out in the Spirit, and even the hardships of life if patiently borne—all of these become spiritual sacrifices acceptable to God through Jesus Christ.'"[2]

This is an important realization for us who are living the Christian vocation to family life; who daily sacrifice our time so that we can do honest work well; who give up our best hours in order to raise our children, comfort our friends and care for our ailing parents. For those are our spiritual sacrifices. And we mustn't underestimate their value. The Second Vatican Council declared: "During the celebration of the Eucharist, these sacrifices are most lovingly offered to the Father along with the Lord's body. Thus, as worshipers whose every deed is holy, the laity consecrate the world itself to God."[3]

That's a powerful notion: that our everyday works, joys and aggravations are our own priestly participation in the Mass. Reading these passages should change the way we look upon Mass and in turn should change the way we live. What is the quality of the gifts we place on the altar? To what degree can I truthfully call myself a worshiper "whose every deed is holy"?

Our priesthood should call us to a deep examination of conscience. For when we sin—when we gossip, vent anger or detract from another's reputation—we are abusing our priesthood; we are placing unseemly gifts on the altar with the Body of the Lord.

We wouldn't stand idly by while our parish priests made such an offering. We should hold our own priesthood to the same high standard.

ELEVEN

Work Hard, Mary!

My wife felt terrible dropping me off at the emergency room. But what else could she do? It was late at night. We have no family living nearby. And she had five small children to tend, all of them shocked to see their father writhing in pain in the front of the van.

At the hospital's emergency entrance, I staggered out of the van and waved the family on. An attendant helped me into a wheelchair and rolled me in.

I told the triage nurse my symptoms, chief of which was severe abdominal and back pain—the worst I'd ever known. She nodded and said, "Flu. Everybody's got the flu. Not much we can do for it."

I felt fairly sure it wasn't the flu, but I'm a docile patient. The attendant put me on a gurney and rolled me into a hallway lined with gurneys, each occupied by a patient who obviously had the flu. It was going to be a long night.

And a dark and stormy one, at least in my body and soul. The pain came in waves that, at least three times, knocked me off the gurney and onto the floor. I remembered a dear friend of mine, a neurologist, giving a talk on pain, explaining that pain comes to occupy the entire consciousness of the patient. Yes, yes, yes, I thought.

The only other thought my mind could form was that I

wanted to be mothered. OK, I'm a grown man, but I'm not ashamed to say it: I wanted my mommy.

Alas, she was several hundred miles away. And as I said, my wife, who is no slouch at mothering, was home with the little ones.

I still had one maternal option to try. I reached into my pocket and pulled out my rosary. Over the three hours I spent in that hallway, I managed to get through five decades. It was Monday—the Joyful Mysteries.

The pain ended abruptly when I saw a doctor, who pronounced me afflicted not with the flu but with kidney stones. He gave me a narcotic, which gave me sweet sleep. I spent the night in the hospital and returned home in the morning. And, of course, I called my mom.

The next few days I spent on the couch, dosed with painkillers. Meanwhile the kids managed to contract chicken pox, a stomach virus and a respiratory bug. Then we got word that my mom was rushed to the hospital and would need surgery.

Mom has often told me the story of her own mother's final illness. My grandmother's last words to her teenage daughter were, "Work hard, Mary."

In the difficult days of my stones—days that stretched into weeks—I took my grandmother's words as my prayer to the Mother of God. For my mom, as she undergoes surgery—work hard, Mary! For my kids, as they itch with the pox—work hard, Mary! For my own surgery to blast the stones—work hard, Mary!

I meant no impertinence. Coming as they do from my grandmother via my mom, those words carry much maternal authority—which is just the sort of authority we attribute to "Mother Church."

TWELVE

Pulling the Wool Over

In 2002 my dad injured his back and had an extended stay at the hospital where my sister Florence is an administrator. It was amusing for me to visit Pop and watch people scurry whenever my big sister turned the corner. I wanted to explain to the cowering multitude that Florence is really harmless. But I thought it best not to blow her cover.

Florence regularly stopped in to make sure Pop was getting what he needed. One day she arrived just as a doctor was starting a routine exam. When my father took off his shirt, the doctor lifted up the brown Marian image that draped from a string at Pop's chest. Under orders from my mother, no doubt, he long had worn the brown scapular, the woolen badge of devotion to Our Lady of Mount Carmel.

"I used to wear one of these!" the doctor said. "Where can I get one?"

My mom volunteered to bring one in the next day.

"Ooh, I'd like one too," chimed in the nurse who was helping.

Mom—who kept a regiment's supply at home at all times—said she'd bring a bagful.

And so she did. Arriving at Pop's bedside bright and early the next morning, Mom asked Florence to let the doctor and nurse know that their scapular shipment had arrived.

Florence returned to the corridor, and once again employees scurried in her wake. At the nurses' station she stopped and peeked in, ever so briefly. "My father has your scapulars," she said. And she was gone, on to the elevator.

Later on Florence told us that she'd arrived in her office just in time to answer the ringing phone.

It was the nurse upstairs.

"Um, Florence," the nurse said sheepishly, "what exactly am I supposed to do to your father's scapula?"

The scapula, as any nurse can tell you, is the flat bone at the back of the shoulder. The brown scapular is named for the scapula bone, against which its mantle rests. Florence, who can evangelize as intensely as she does everything else, was able to explain the difference.

Well, no matter where we go, God gives us opportunities to share our faith. Pop did his part; so did Mom; so did Flo.

The scapular is a sign of filial devotion and of a commitment to living the kind of discipleship that Mary lived. Those who wear the scapular strive to serve as Mary did.

They also strive to spread the devotion. And I guess that's what I'm doing as I type up this particular page. If you're not already wearing a scapular, start now. If you are wearing one, find out how many of your friends and family members might like to do the same. Do unto others as my mom and pop did for their doctor and nurse.

And do as Florence did for her colleague: explain the devotion to those who might misunderstand. It's not superstition, any more than the family photos in my wallet or the word "Mom" I saw tattooed on a man's arm at the grocery store today. It's all about family, and it's all for love.

THIRTEEN

D.C. Talk

I was prepared for a penitential period. I was, after all, scheduled to spend three days in midsummer with my son's Boy Scout troop, hiking thirty-six miles of urban trails through Washington, D.C., our populous and humid national capital—which, incidentally, is built on a swamp. There would be mosquitoes abuzz and a throng of preteen boys with the usual aversion to hygiene.

The weather lived up to the weatherman's promises. Every day the heat index climbed over a hundred as the boys trudged on. I considered it my duty to keep the kids hydrated. I spent a small fortune buying Gatorade from street vendors.

We wove our way past hundreds of statues, memorials and plaques celebrating the country's founders, its war dead, its leaders. My son, knowing that such sights might inspire me to reverie, kept his distance, lest I should begin a nerdy history lecture in the presence of his buddies. I mused on anyway but silently.

I was struck by the grandeur of the city's architecture. We Americans tend to build our churches plain and functional, while we spare no cost for our civic monuments. We build for eternity, with granite and marble laid, block upon block, in colossal imitation of the ancient temples of Europe and Egypt.

And just as the ancient pagans celebrated the deeds of Hercules and Augustus, so we Americans have built stunning shrines to Washington, Jefferson and Lincoln. Awestruck visitors from all around the world instinctively speak in hushed tones when they walk amid the colonnades. Indeed, the National Park Service posts signs *urging* tourists to keep a reverent silence.

I willingly comply. Before the genius of Jefferson, the courage of Washington and the wisdom of Lincoln, I stand quite naturally in awe.

Yet everywhere we toured I was struck by the fundamental paganism of our civic religion. George Washington dedicated the Capitol building not with a Christian benediction but with a Masonic ritual involving a sacrificial ox and a silver plate. Jefferson labored over an edition of the New Testament that removed all references to Jesus' divinity and miracles. Lincoln, though a churchgoer, could not bring himself to believe in Christianity.

Still, I love these men for the country they built; and at every memorial I prayed for the repose of their souls—especially Lincoln's, because I love him the most and in spite of his flaws.

For me the most garish expression of our civic religion is the "Apotheosis of Washington," the centerpiece mural in the Capitol building, which depicts the first president as a sort of Christ in a powdered wig, ascended to glory, surrounded by angels. I grew gloomy beneath that mural, especially as I mused upon the issues that beset the Capitol building in our day: cloning, abortion, assisted suicide, stem cell research. I stepped quickly to refuge in the statuary hall, where I suspected my son had ducked away.

And what a refuge I found. The room was cluttered with heroic marbles of mostly muscular men, done up in the Greek style. A single bronze, easily the most dynamic statue in the room, dominated that bloodless crowd. It was Blessed Junípero Serra, the apostle to California, and he held high—high above the heads of his historic fellows—a large cross. All I could say was, "Wow!" and, "Amen," as my eyes welled up.

There in the statuary hall, I prayed my most fervent prayer. I asked for that great man's intercession, and I prayed that the holy cross might redeem our time and our country's history.

Fourteen

The Chainsaw Denied

Every now and then I pick up a phrase wafting from a nearby conversation, and it sticks with me.

When we were newlyweds Terri and I were eating at a fast-food restaurant. At a table across the aisle sat a weary mother and her talkative and obviously precocious five-year-old. The patter of their conversation (especially his portion) ran non-stop as an accompaniment to our own. But only one line managed to push past our mental filters. In the most earnest maternal voice, the mom said to the five-year-old, "And just where do you suppose you'll get this chainsaw?"

Terri and I looked at each other and tried to suppress our laughter. For some time afterward we tried to imagine the context of that mother's question. Had low-budget horror flicks about Texas massacres inspired the boy? Had he issued a threat? Did he want to build the family a log cabin? Or was he an aspiring postmodern artist seeking a government grant to destroy furniture?

Though we hadn't heard the boy's request, there was something so psychologically true about the mother's deadpan question. Every mother knows that children believe they have a right to fulfillment of their every whim and wish. To kids parents seem obtuse or cruel when they deny things that, to Mom and Dad, are clearly unsafe, unhealthy or immoral—like a seventh helping of candy or retribution visited upon a younger sibling or the possession of a chainsaw.

As we grow we put away such childish wishes. Only craftsmen, woodsmen, hobbyists and true psychopaths continue to hanker after a chainsaw. But we never quite outgrow the belief that we have a right to the things we so clearly see as good for us: *this* job, a home in *that* neighborhood, a complete healing or a lasting experience of human love. Like the little boy in the restaurant, we fume and we rail at God when he doesn't grant our requests in just the way we want them.

God knows when something we urgently desire would, over the long haul, lead to our everlasting destruction—when an apparently good thing would lead to situations that are unsafe, unhealthy or immoral for us. Only in retrospect (and sometimes not even then) can we see that the things God denied us were things that could have harmed us: a particular job or spouse or home. Only with wisdom do we see that even our privations are gifts from a God who wants our happiness. We imagine a content and productive life with our chainsaw (or whatever); he sees the certain carnage that would ensue.

God provides even when his denial seems most severe. Out of the desolate ground of the Nazi concentration camps—where so many prayers seemed to go unanswered—grew lavish flowers of holiness: in Edith Stein, Maximilian Kolbe, Titus Brandsma and countless others.

Part of growing up spiritually is learning to be grateful for all things, even our difficulties, disappointments, failures and humiliations. "We know that in everything God works for good with those who love him" (Romans 8:28).

FIFTEEN

Felines, Phobias and Faults

From the start of this chapter, I apologize to all cat lovers, cat owners and even those who are merely kind, in a Franciscan way, to such creatures. I pray your patience. For I confess: I have a singular loathing for all things feline, a dread of cat presence, a deep-seated belief that, as a species, cats participate in a vast plot to bring about my demise. Call me irrational, but "the heart has its reasons, which reason does not know."[1]

When I was in college, I dated a girl whose cat would hiss at me from the moment I entered her family home. One night Kitty's hissing seemed excessive, even for a creature so low on the great chain of being. I kept up my end of the parlor chitchat, always watching the creature out of the corner of my eye. For a moment I must have turned away, and he saw his chance. Suddenly I felt claws digging into the skin on my neck. And there was Kitty, tearing at my flesh, having lunged from a nearby lamp stand.

Within minutes my neck began to swell. A number of allergies had struck me just before adolescence, when my body chemistry was going haywire. And of all those teenage allergies, only one has survived into my adulthood—and severely. You guessed which one.

For many years my in-laws owned a cat, and all of Terri's sisters still do, which makes visits difficult. Even if I douse my system with antihistamines, I eventually get a suffocating feeling, as if the air's being sucked out of the house. When I stayed with my in-laws—whom I dearly love—I was seized by urges I had at no other times: to go to the mall, to take long walks in a nearby cemetery, to run to the convenience store to buy milk (so what if Mom didn't need any?).

My feline fright was much with me several years ago when my wife found a dream home for us to inhabit. Terri and I had been house hunting for more than a year, and the place we kept coming back to was the current residence of a cat (and sometimes two cats). Now, that little tom had shown no particular animosity toward me and had made no wild lunges for my jugular. Yet as we were browsing the rooms of the house, I felt the old familiar feeling: the breathable air draining away around me, like bathwater running out of the tub.

But buying the house had been ordained, if not from eternity, at least for a long time and by an authority that is great upon the earth—that is, my wife's. So as we closed in on the purchase, I concluded that God was trying to teach me something important through his creatures.

My feline phobia is, I think, something like the horror I'm supposed to feel for sin—not just mortal sin but any sin. The saints and spiritual masters write about such a horror and pray for it. I haven't known it well enough, and I find that I make the same confessions week after week and go months without feeling any aversion in conscience that I might compare to my loathing for cats. In spite of an abundance of sacramental graces, I find myself ambling sleepily into my by now routine sins.

If only I had a suffocating feeling whenever I approached a sinful thought, word, deed or omission. If only my neck swelled upon each occasion of impatience with the kids, insensitivity toward my wife or anger toward those I perceive as enemies. If only my urges to criticize others could be automatically overwhelmed by the desire to see a shopping mall or for some other severe mortification. If only I could see that, while it's irrational to believe in a feline conspiracy to make me sneeze, it's the height of sanity to believe in a vast demonic conspiracy to make me sin.

If only, if only...

Though I'd give much to lose my cat allergy—to have normal visits with Terri's family, to wish the good of even the least of God's creatures—I'd give even more to gain that sin allergy. I'm told that it comes with time, with regular confession and with diligence in personal prayer. In the meantime I hear in my heart the promise God made to Saint Paul, when the apostle prayed for deliverance from sin (not cats): "My grace is sufficient for you, for my power is made perfect in weakness" (2 Corinthians 12:9).

I've got to believe that that stuff works better than antihistamines.

Sixteen

What Are We Waiting For?

I hate to stand in line. I hate to be put on hold. I hate to be kept waiting in front of the movie theater when I come to pick up my preteen kids and their friends. And even now, as I type late at night, I am dreading the inches-per-hour traffic I'll encounter tomorrow as I try to enter the city at rush hour.

I'm a normal, busy American who's always in a hurry to get somewhere—to work, to a doctor's appointment, home. I have plans. Like every red-blooded American hurrier, I view time in queue as time lost. I could be doing something with that time.

This is not just a hunch. I've had this intuition confirmed for me by Experts Who Know Better. Back when I worked in a corporation, I learned from the best-dressed consultants that "queue time" is the great enemy of efficiency.

Christmas shopping season (what the church calls Advent) is the worst season for my sort of American. The lines are longer in the stores. The traffic is worse. Whenever I'm placed on hold, the phone seems to play "The Little Drummer Boy" on an infinite tape loop. And my kids insist on being driven to stores where they can spend hours agonizing over the purchase of gifts, while I—so as not to spoil any surprises—am exiled to the frozen car.

My first instinct is to look for a demonic origin for all this, but that's not right. Nothing comes from Satan but lies, and somehow all of these nuisances are true, faithful to the facts of the season.

Our frenetic, materialist society—through God's providence —has evolved a month of anxious and seemingly interminable waiting before Christmas. Surely this is a sign of the times. Surely God has given (or at least allowed) these conditions in order to teach us the truth about Advent.

Advent is a time when we should dip a little bit more into the Old Testament, especially the prophets, to learn what it's really like to wait and wait and wait—for centuries. Sometimes, perhaps, it can be hard for us to sympathize with the chosen people, because we read the prophetic books backward, knowing their fulfillment in Jesus. But during Advent we should exercise our imaginations a little more and put ourselves in the place of the pious Israelites who longed for the day of the Messiah's coming—knowing not when or where or how exactly it would happen, but wanting it right then. Their recurring refrain was, "How long, Lord? How long?"

This is an opportunity many of us miss in Advent. For many commuters the seasonal traffic seems to inspire little more than obscene gestures.

We can live in our anxious time as the Old Testament prophets lived in theirs. They believed in God's promise and in God's law. This faith gave them a fine sensitivity to injustice and a holy impatience for the day of the Lord's coming. Once we have sanctified our impatience, we can use it to fuel our tireless work to advance the coming of the kingdom.

Maybe we can use our time in line or on hold or in the car to pray to God or to dream up an act of charity. It's Advent, after all. And what are we waiting for?

SEVENTEEN

It's All I Do

My name is Mike, and I'm a latent workaholic. I say "latent" because my wife won't have it any other way—thank God for that.

I caught a glimpse of my tendencies last summer when Terri took the kids to visit her parents for a week. While they were away I hardly left my desk, working through mealtimes, worrying over details of page after page I was writing, staring for long hours into the blue glow of my computer screen.

With the kids away I should have had more time to give to prayer. But my obsessive labors consumed the moments. Only nature's more insistent calls could force me from my desk. Supernature is far too gentle.

Far too gentle indeed. When the family came home, I noticed that I sustained my workaholism even when appearing not to. While nodding at the ramblings of my four-year-old, I was mentally composing a newspaper column. While fingering my rosary, my mind veered from the Joyful Mysteries to the tedium of expense reports and correspondence. I am single-minded but not for the "one thing...needful" (Luke 10:42).

How I wish my children would be able to remember someday their childhood the way I remember mine.

My father was a single-minded man, and I've known no more diligent worker in my lifetime. When I was very small, he worked on heavy machinery as a mechanic for a coal company.

Sometimes his work took him on long commutes from home, and he didn't get back until nightfall. He was exhausted and dusty, and surely he had earned a moment to himself, to read the paper or channel-surf or just collapse on the couch. But all that he showed me was his eagerness to play.

As I said earlier, some of my earliest memories are of that beautiful man—fifty-two years old when I was five—falling asleep under me as we wrestled on the floor. His every waking moment, it seemed to me, was given to love for his family.

Saint John of the Cross wrote of this single-mindedness in his "Spiritual Canticle":

> I gave my heart and soul. My fortune too.
>   I've no flock any more,
>   no other work in view.
>   My occupation: love. It's all I do.[1]

Perhaps we don't attain this love by leaving our "flocks" and other labors altogether but by having the same mind and heart when we are at work as we do when we are gazing into the eyes of our neighbors or our children. Only one thing is needful, and it's not work. It's love. "It's all I do," said Saint John.

Workaholics like me need to learn to "leave God for God," as Saint Vincent de Paul and many other saints have expressed it. We need to turn from our God-given responsibilities at the computer screen to the faces of those around us. We need to work only for love, so we'll know when to leave work behind.

EIGHTEEN

Dadolatry

I have to admit that I love Daddy worship. The stage varies in duration, but so far all my kids have gone through it. It begins the first time they realize that someone besides Mom is committed to unconditionally loving Baby. And it soon develops into the belief that Dad is all-knowing, all-loving and all-powerful.

But, alas, Daddy worship must come to an end. In our home it seems to cease when a two- or three-year-old approaches me with a smashed, beloved toy in hand, eyes alight with hope that surely such a great god can heal all things. My temptation then is to do something spectacular. "Listen, I'll buy you a better toy, one packed with gadgetry and labeled with a hundred-dollar price tag."

But that's not right. This is the time when Dad's vocation as Dad really kicks in. In lieu of miracles, he can offer his open arms.

The temptation is always there, no matter what one's vocation may be, to do something outlandish, to manifest one's spiritual gifts publicly for reasons of personal pride. The devil knows this weakness, and that's why he dared Jesus again and again to make a spectacle of himself, to *prove* that he was the Son of God (see Luke 4:3, 9).

The notion perhaps gets reinforcement today from some well-intentioned editions of the lives of the saints. In chapter after chapter we readers are dazzled with the miraculous, the mystical, the extraordinary. By page twenty-eight we're pretty sure that *we're* not supposed to be saints, because our lives are so very ordinary. Nothing particularly miraculous, no cures, no ecstatic visions—just day after day of hard work, occasional moments of leisure and up-and-down family life.

Yet that is precisely the stuff of sanctity. And *that* is the message of Saint Thérèse of Lisieux, the doctor of the church who offered the world a "little way" to holiness. She wrote that "little things done out of love" are those that charm the heart of Christ. On the other hand, "without love even the most brilliant deeds count for nothing."[1] Elsewhere she said of her own life: "All I did was to break my self-will, check a hasty reply and do little kindnesses without making a fuss."[2] Her life was lowly by any standard. Yet she has been exalted in her afterlife as very few saints have been exalted in all of history.

Imagine if we could live Thérèse's "little way" at work, at home, at play. Well, imagine that, and you've imagined the kingdom of God.

Thérèse's way of littleness marks great holiness. As we diminish, as we deny ourselves, then Christ's life grows where our own has been. "It is no longer I who live," Saint Paul said, "but Christ who lives in me" (Galatians 2:20). When we've so diminished ourselves that we're practically selfless, that's when Christ truly reigns in our hearts. This is among the most ancient Christian truths: "He must increase, but I must decrease" (John 3:30).

I remember once, as I was working, I overheard my seven-year-old son in the hallway trying to console his four-year-old sister, who was sulking over one of his unintended insults. He offered her "the whole Milky Way galaxy" if she would just play with him again. I'm sure he'd give her the galaxy if he could.

But you and I know that his holiness must come some other way, some little way.

NINETEEN

Lego Pain

It was an ill omen. Dawn's early light was still at least an hour away. Since the two youngest girls had interrupted my sleep twice apiece, the buzzing of my alarm clock seemed a gross injustice. But we must face these things courageously. So I sat up, muttered a Morning Offering and took my stand, planting my foot firmly onto a Lego toy.

Now, for those of you who are uninitiated, Legos are plastic building blocks designed by top engineers in Sweden for one purpose only: to inflict pain upon parents who inadvertently step on them. They're just small enough to be invisible to a man who can't find his glasses, just hard and sharp enough to damage a nerve without puncturing paternal skin.

In my childhood low-tech metal jacks served the same purpose. Then some bright mom with a degree in polymer science advanced the cause of humanity by inventing bendable rubber jacks. But ever since our first parents decided to taste the forbidden fruit, the universe must obey an inexorable Law of the Conservation of Parental Pain. And so the cosmos demanded Legos for me to step on.

As I said, it all seemed an ill omen: the insufficient sleep, the annoying alarm, the Lego pain. Surely it would be a wicked day. I contemplated that thought as I trudged downstairs to put coffee on, and I developed it even more fully as the coffee brewed. Whereupon I trudged back upstairs to wake my wife to her own share in the inevitable misery.

But I stepped back into the dim room to see two tiny eyes looking back at me from the bed. Grace Marie, who was then fourteen months old, was just waking up, her face still expressionless as she processed what she saw.

Can toddlers sense a day that began with Lego pain? How perceptive could she be? Maybe more perceptive than a grumpy grown-up. "Daddy!" she shouted suddenly, with the biggest smile you can imagine.

And my foot felt fine. What a gorgeous day it would be! The sun was beginning to peek in through the bedroom blinds.

In my proudest moments I believe in the greatness that Gracie's smile seems to acknowledge. I believe that my glorious and awesome presence can make all the difference in a baby's day or anyone else's, should they possess such precocious powers of perception as Gracie has.

But in my most honest moments, I know that my fatherhood is just a dim reflection of the *only* true fatherhood, which belongs to God. Gracie's smile teaches me the joy and confidence I should feel as a true child of God my Father, who is King of the universe I live in and who loves me with a lasting and merciful love—even though the things I leave lying around are sometimes much nastier than Legos.

TWENTY

Question Authority

I like question-and-answer catechisms. The good sisters taught me from the *Baltimore Catechism* for the first five years of my schooling, and I'm always surprised at how many of those rote answers I've retained from my otherwise misspent school years.

I like the question-and-answer format because it mimics the way we approach life. We humans are inquisitive creatures. Sometimes, when we come up with urgent questions, it's good to have a plausible answer at hand. When we're in the dumps and we ask ourselves, *Why ever did God make me?* it helps immensely to know the reason.

We haven't dusted off the old *Baltimore Catechism* for our children, but we do try to teach them by Q&A. When our Rosemary was three, she and I could rattle off a series in seconds flat.

Dad: Who made you?
Rosemary: God!
Dad: And why did God make you?
Rosemary: To be a great saint!

She always passed the test, which meant that I picked her up and spun her around, marveling at her brilliance.

Now, some people would complain that that was just mechanical learning, but I know otherwise. One Sunday morning Rosemary came down the steps dressed for Mass in a gorgeous new outfit. I did a double take, lifted her high and said to her, "Why are you so cute?"

Rosemary hesitated, then dutifully answered, "Because God wants me to be a great *and cute* saint."

I hadn't meant the question to be a quiz, but she took it that way, and she passed with flying colors. She grasped what the church calls the "universal call to holiness."

God made me to be a great saint. No matter what other words I use to describe myself ("cute" wouldn't be one of them), they should fit that sentence neatly. No task I perform, no quality of my personality, no pastime I enjoy, should be out of place in the life of a saint. "Be perfect," Jesus said, "as your heavenly Father is perfect" (Matthew 5:48). Saint Matthew makes it clear that Jesus was speaking here not to his clergy but to "the crowd" (see Matthew 7:28). He was speaking to husbands, wives and children, calling them all to be saints.

This is an easy lesson to forget. We're conditioned to think of saints as odd folks indeed, taking our cues from low-budget statues and simpering holy cards. We can get so caught up in the spectacular events in saints' lives that we forget that their call is our call. The saints are an odd assortment, but no odder a mix than you and I.

This is what Rosemary knows and what you and I must strive to learn, one question at a time.

TWENTY-ONE

For the Love of Coffee

I'm a coffee drinker.

No, strike that. I love coffee: the sound of its brewing, the smell, the warmth and, of course, the taste. I love it.

I can hear all the nuns from my years in Catholic school chorusing that I should *never, ever* say that I love anything but people and God. And I admit they're right, as usual. But I *do* love coffee. It is for me what the spiritual masters call a "disordered attachment," and one of these days I'll have to get around to giving it up.

I'm comforted somewhat by knowing that coffee was the last attachment of the great Dorothy Day, the Servant of God whose birthday I share. The story goes that she carried packets of instant around in her purse just in case her host ran out of brew. None of this eluded the notice of her spiritual director, Father John Hugo, who recorded it for posterity. I'm sure that both Dorothy and Father Hugo are spinning in their holy graves as I take comfort in their words, because I know (the sisters taught me) that the disordered attachment to worldly things is as wrong for me as it was for Dorothy Day.

Not that coffee is the "devil's brew," as some Spanish prelates claimed a few centuries ago. It's a very good creation of a very good God. The trouble with coffee—or rather with me—is that it's the first thing I think of when I roll out of bed and fall on my alarm clock in the morning. My Morning

Offering may be muddled and mumbled, but I'm frightfully clearheaded about the route to the coffeemaker and the precise measurement of the grounds.

The good thing about Lent is that it makes such matters very clear to us. What are the things we place before God? What takes precedence over him when the alarm goes off? What comes to mind when we're running a little bit late for dinner? Saint Paul spoke of those folks whose God is their belly (see Philippians 3:19), and I'm sure he meant me when my body's crying out for a caffeine fix.

During Lent we pray, fast and give alms with more care, more love and more intensity than we do during the rest of the year. All these practices help us draw closer to the Lord, as we sweep aside things that separate us from him. Again, all the good things in life—desserts, sex, leisure and sleep—are good because God made them. The problem isn't with the things of this world but with our weak and fickle wills.

So maybe I won't fill the pot so often this Lent. Maybe now and then I can make an attentive morning prayer anyway. And when I do get the urge to top off the mug, maybe I'll take it as God's reminder to do something nice for my dear wife and kids, my neighbors and my coworkers. As I love *them* more, for God's sake, maybe I'll love coffee just a little less and God a whole lot more.

TWENTY-TWO

The Joy of Fasting

Why do Catholics have to fast?"

The question came, with an implicit complaint, from one of my son's buddies, a Boy Scout in our troop. We had spent a long, soggy weekend in the middle of the woods. And now, Sunday morning, the adults announced that breakfast would be delayed so that the Catholics could keep the Communion fast. Little Bobby, who is not Catholic, was *not* a happy camper.

Every year Bobby's question returns to my mind as Lent begins, because fasting is the most distinguishing practice of the season. On two days in Lent, Ash Wednesday and Good Friday, Catholics limit their eating to one full meatless meal. On all the Fridays of Lent we abstain from meat. That's the extent of our required fasting, but I have to admit that it's not a practice I particularly enjoy. In fact, when Lent rolls around I can whine with Bobby, an otherwise admirable Boy Scout:"Why do we have to fast?"

Our reasons find firm grounding in the Bible. When we fast we follow holy example. Moses and Elijah fasted forty days before going into God's presence (see Exodus 34:28; 1 Kings 19:8). Anna the prophetess fasted to prepare herself for the coming of the Messiah (Luke 2:37).They all wanted to see God, and they considered fasting a basic prerequisite. We, too, wish to enter God's presence, so we fast.

Jesus fasted (see Matthew 4:2). And since he needed no purification, he surely did this only to set an example for us. In fact, he assumed that all Christians would follow his example. "When you fast," he said, "do not look dismal, like the hypocrites, for they disfigure their faces that their fasting may be seen by men" (Matthew 6:16). Note that he did not say, "*If* you fast" but "*When.*"

In Lent the church extends the idea of fasting beyond the minimal skipping of meals to a more far-reaching program of self-denial. Jesus said: "If any man would come after me, let him deny himself...daily" (Luke 9:23). So we "give up" something that we enjoy: sweets, soda pop, a favorite TV show or the snooze alarm.

Fasting has its health benefits, but it's not the same as dieting. Fasting is something spiritual and far more positive. It is a spiritual feast. It does for the soul what food does for the body.

The Bible spells out specific spiritual benefits of fasting. It produces humility (see Psalm 69:10). It shows our sorrow for our sins (1 Samuel 7:6). It clears a path to God (Daniel 9:3). It is a means of discerning God's will and a powerful method of prayer (Ezra 8:21, 23). It's a mark of true conversion (Joel 2:12).

Fasting helps us to be detached from the things of this world. We fast not because earthly things are evil but precisely because they're good, so good that we sometimes prefer them to the Giver.

We often prefer self-indulgence to self-denial. We tend to eat and drink to the point where we forget God. Such indulgence is really a form of idolatry. Again, remember those words of Saint Paul, "Their god is the belly,...with minds set on earthly things" (Philippians 3:19).

How can we enjoy God's gifts without forgetting the Giver? Fasting is a good way to start. The body wants more than it needs, so we should give it less than it wants.

Saint John of the Cross said that we cannot rise up to God if we are bound to the things of this world. So we give up good things, and gradually we grow less dependent on them, less needy.

All of this is part of our preparation for heaven. For we're destined to lose our earthly goods anyway. Time, age, illness and "doctor's orders" can take away the taste for chocolate, the ability to enjoy a cold beer and even the intimate embrace of a spouse. If we have no discipline over our desires, then those losses will leave us bitter and estranged from God. But if we follow Jesus in self-denial, we'll find a more habitual consolation in the ultimate good, God himself.

How is it that some people are able to remain serene and cheerful amid extreme suffering and even when facing imminent death? It's not just a matter of temperament. They've prepared themselves for the moment by giving up the things of this world, one small thing at a time. They've grown so accustomed to small sacrifices that the big one isn't such a stretch.

When people die that way, their families find immediate consolation. I was startled to hear from my sister Mary that my dad had told her, shortly before his death, that he was "ready to go." All my life I could not imagine his going without a fight, because death would mean separation from my mom. For him to go willingly meant that he had achieved a heroic degree of detachment. He accomplished this by grace through suffering and self-denial, which included, of course, keeping the fasts the church required.

Why do Catholics have to fast? God doesn't need our fasting, but God knows we need it. We need to fast, and we need it more than we need all the good things we're giving up.

TWENTY-THREE

Values Clarification

The seventies were a bizarre time to go to high school, no matter where you went. The winds of change seemed to whip a new educational trend down the corridors every week.

Mine was a good Catholic school run by an excellent order of sisters, so my classmates and I were spared much of the silliness. We did arrive one September to find an "Awareness Room" with throw pillows on the floor and Ziggy posters on the walls. But human nature being what it is, we high-schoolers enjoyed the room's silliness to the limit, and the sisters closed off our Awareness before the year was done.

That experiment was an exception to the sisters' Golden Rule of teaching. For the most part they taught unto us the way they would have anyone teach unto them.

Back in my middle-school years, values clarification was hot, and one of my lay teachers decided to try it on me and my peers. Miss Earnestine (not her real name) was fresh out of an undergrad education major and actually excited about this stuff. She opened our discussion with the classic lifeboat drill, and we entered into it with the enthusiasm we ordinarily reserved for health-class lectures on hand-washing.

Our ship had sunk, she explained, and fifteen of us were clinging to a lifeboat that only had room for ten. Which people would we allow on board? Which would we doom to a watery grave?

She sketched profiles of the competition: a doctor, a professor of literature, a woman paralyzed from the waist down, her lawyer husband, a seventy-year-old carpenter,...you get the idea. We were supposed to determine the value of each person to our community of survivors.

We groaned our way through the exercise. Our teacher was disappointed. She said that we had to consider these matters, that they were important.

Then she moved on to situation number two: "You and your family are in a concentration camp," she said. "The guard tells you that you must choose which one of your parents will survive and which will be shot. Whom do you choose?"

Now, a confession is in order. I was not a good student. I wasn't a delinquent, but I was a know-it-all and what one nun called a "lazy lump." Still, situation number two was too much for me. And whom did Miss Earnestine choose to call on first?

"No," I said.

"No?" she replied, astonished.

"No. I won't answer. This is stupid."

"You have to answer. This is important."

"It's not, and I won't."

We had pushed the argument to first principles. And that's when my values really got clarified.

She walked to my desk, crossed her arms and squinted down at me. "You will because I said so."

I squinted right back and shook my head.

She smiled. "Would you like to talk to the principal about it?"

And then I received what only can be called a revelation. I could clearly picture the conference with Sister Principal. I could see my teacher trying to explain the concentration-camp dilemma under Sister's increasingly incredulous stare. I mean, what could they do? Call my parents in to *make* me choose which one to snuff?

So I took up her challenge: "Sure," I said as I stood up and walked toward the door.

I could see by her eyes that my teacher was receiving the same revelation, imagining the same scene with the same ending: the firing of a young, earnest laywoman. She squinted again, this time really hard.

"Sit. Down," she said.

By then, I believe, it was time for math. I slumped back into the anonymity of a lazy lump, and so I remain. But at least I can say with confidence that for one brief moment long ago, my values, a teacher's values and the eternal truths were clarified perfectly for me.

TWENTY-FOUR

The State of Grace

A lone blonde in a crowd of brunettes, our Grace Marie early sensed her difference, her distinctiveness.

One October night the family poured out of the van and approached our favorite ice cream parlor, now decorated for the harvest season. Suddenly three-year-old Gracie broke ranks and ran to a pair of scarecrows.

"Look, Mom! Look, Mom! Look, Mom!"

She jumped repeatedly in front of the floppy couple. We all looked but couldn't figure out what was so special. She pointed emphatically to the golden straw peeking out from the scarecrows' hats. "Look! Gracie dolls!"

Our peerless blonde had found her peers, or at least she thought so. I found them entirely too subdued to pass for "Gracie dolls."

Early in Gracie's life I decided that the word *irrepressible* must have been coined for her. From the time she could crawl, she's had boundless energy and an inquisitive mind. She could jump without ceasing while she asked a breathless series of questions: "What are eyelashes for? Why did God make dinosaurs? How do flowers know what colors to turn?"

In exhausted prayer I would suggest to our Lord that perhaps he should have sent Gracie when I was twenty-five rather than thirty-five. But if he had, I now would have even less muscle in my abdomen than the little I can claim. Gracie is extremely affectionate, and from toddlerhood on her preferred display of affection has been the flying leap. (Ballet lessons have only made her more adept at this.) So I've grown accustomed to tensing my abdomen, just in case it should have to absorb a strong and sudden impact. I'd wager that, even as I sleep, my belly stays as taut as it can, just in case Gracie should swoop in from some dark corner of the master bedroom.

When our family flew to Rome several years ago, Gracie was only five, and she could barely contain her excitement. As our jetliner passed over the ocean, she bounced across the aisles, from sibling to sibling in the Aquilina dispersion, back to her parents, then back through the cycle.

Shortly after landing, through an unpredictable series of events, we found our jet-lagged selves at Pope John Paul II's regular Wednesday audience, with passes to greet the pope personally afterward. Everyone in the family was awestruck by the presence of that great man, now stooped and partially paralyzed from age and ailments. One by one we passed before him. He hugged each of the children. But none of us had the courage or presence of mind to say anything, except, of course, Gracie, who hugged him tight and said, "I love you very much." The flashing cameras captured his broad smile forever, and hers.

Later, back at the hotel, we experienced the comedown from the excitement of meeting a pope and a saint. Factor in the time difference between Rome and Pittsburgh, and we were plummeting toward collapse. Everyone headed to a room and found a place on a bed, a comfy chair or the floor. I dropped to a mattress, so utterly exhausted that it never occurred to me that I was leaving my abdomen wide open.

Sure enough, as soon as I closed my eyes—*crash, whoosh,* and out went the breath from my lungs. There was Gracie hovering over my face, smiling what her mother calls her "thousand-watt smile."

"Oh, honey," I groaned, "if you'll just let me sleep five minutes, I'll be a new man when I wake up."

And then I saw something I had never seen before. Gracie, looking frightened, jumped off me as suddenly as she'd landed. She turned to Terri: "Mommy, when Daddy's a new man..."

"Yes?"

"When Daddy's a new man, what will he look like?"

All the kids erupted in laughter, but Terri just hugged our actual Grace and said, "Remember what the pope looked like?"

Gracie nodded.

"He'll look like that."

Gracie accepted this and let me have my forty winks.

The *Catechism of the Catholic Church* defines grace as "a participation in the life of God" (*CCC*, 1997). What is God's life? Boundless joy, boundless love, limitless energy, unceasing wonder.

God gives us the grace we need when we need it. He gives us the children we need just when we need them. He has given me Grace, amazing Grace, abundantly.

TWENTY-FIVE

Roman Holy Day

For the week of our pilgrimage in Rome, our family of eight crammed into three small rooms at a hotel not far from the Vatican. It was late in the pontificate of Pope John Paul II, and his health was steadily failing, but he still welcomed dozens to join him for the daily Mass in his private chapel. Getting in, though, was not easy.

My preteen son Michael and I were determined to try, egged on by a priest friend who was slated to concelebrate with the pope. We woke up long before dawn and dressed quietly so as not to wake the others. We crept down the hall, down the steps and out into the darkened Roman streets. We shuffled sleepily through city blocks and working-class neighborhoods. The walk passed as quickly as a dream.

When we arrived at the Vatican, first light was just beginning to peek over the old walls. And in that cold morning light, at our final destination, I was able to follow paternal instinct and scan Michael for sartorial aberrations. I almost wished I hadn't.

My eyes fell immediately to his shoes, if you want to call them shoes. My beloved son, my firstborn, had shown up for Mass in the papal apartment wearing sneakers. I pointed this out to him, in those very words.

Michael was mortified. I was worse. I grumbled something about the tragic fate of the improperly dressed wedding guest in the Gospel story (see Matthew 22:11–13). On cue, in a low voice, Michael wailed and gnashed his teeth.

The Swiss Guards didn't notice and, miraculously, admitted us through the bronze doors. After several more checkpoints we wound our way through the corridors of the Vatican to the inner sanctum. It was all happening too easily, again like a dream—except for the sneakers.

Junior ducked into a crowd of nuns at a back corner of the chapel, and he tried his best to hide his ill-shod feet. But the pope's secretary spotted him, and his eyes communicated his thoughts transparently: *A child! The pope loves children!* And then there were my eyes and my thoughts: *Oh, no!*

Bishop Dziwisz beckoned Michael to come forward and sit next to His Holiness. We both gulped, but Michael did as he was told and moved to the seat up front, carefully tucking his feet way, way, way under the chair. From my place in the back, I thought: *What cramps he'll have by the end of this Mass!* And upon a moment's reflection: *He deserves the cramps.*

Afterward, along with the nuns and everyone else in the chapel, we queued up to receive the pope's blessing. Michael and I were both thinking: *Sneakers, sneakers, sneakers.* But Pope John Paul's eyes never even glanced at the ground. Instead he looked my son in the eye with a love that I recognized right away as deeply paternal. He smiled and pronounced the boy's name: "My-koll!" And I almost wished I had shown up in sneakers, too.

Many people call that man John Paul the Great, and perhaps history will as well. From that moment Michael and I knew him as "Papa." I think we always will.

TWENTY-SIX

Love's Language

I don't think my father ever passed up a chance to hold a baby or a small child—or an older child, for that matter (at least on his lap). Some of my earliest memories are of my nephew Jay and me pretending we were asleep at the end of long car rides, so that Pop would carry us into the house. I'm sure he knew we were pretending. I'm sure he didn't mind in the least.

My uncles tell me that Pop had been like that since he was a kid himself. As a teenager he would walk five miles to his older sister's house so that he could walk back home with a baby on his shoulder.

Pop knew the things that delighted us kids, and he kept plenty of them on hand: rolls of Reed's hard candies, packs of Beeman's gum. When I was a kid, he had a spring-loaded keychain that dispensed the nickels he needed for my hometown's notorious parking meters. I think most of those nickels ended up in the pockets of us kids rather than the town coffers.

Pop didn't need to waste a lot of words with us. He was a quiet man, and his shyness grew more pronounced with his deafness. Many of the words he used were his own trademark nonsense, like "ruby jeegy jeeg," which he'd chant endlessly while he walked some baby to sleep. More than once I heard him sing all of Hoagy Carmichael's "Stardust" with "ruby jeegy jeeg" as the only lyrics.

Pop didn't need to express himself in order to give himself. Because after all, it wasn't about him. It was always all about you, whoever you happened to be at the moment. And you *knew* you were his favorite, whether you were his favorite son or daughter, his favorite son-in-law or daughter-in-law, his favorite niece or nephew or grandchild. *You* were the one who mattered.

In 1992, when my daughter Mary Agnes was born, Pop and my mom came to help us out for a few days. Mom cooked up a storm, producing pots of sauce and pans of chicken and loaves of bread. Pop, for his part, paced the floor with the new baby, singing "ruby jeegy Stardust," read to her older brother and found other ways to let Terri and me get some sleep.

I remember one of Pop's rare philosophical moments, when he was pacing with Mary Agnes, who had long since fallen asleep. He said he believed there was a "silent language of love" that passed between adults and children. We didn't need to speak out loud, and they didn't need to learn our expressions.

That little phrase, the "silent language of love," said it all for me. That's the language that my father spoke all the time. He spoke it with my mother as he put icing on hundreds of cookies she'd baked. It's the language that drew my niece Michelle automatically to cuddle with Pop on the couch, even when she was a college student visiting along with her friends.

Pop could use words very effectively, and he could use hard words when we kids earned them. But the silent language of love is the language he used most fluently and most often. It is a comfort to me that he can still speak this today; death is no barrier. My children and I, my siblings and I, my wife and I, still can know Pop's love in the silence.

The kids already know this, of course. The day Pop died they were already preparing his canonization process. Mary Agnes had to run to the store that afternoon, and on the way she asked Poppy in heaven to get the cars to stop and let her cross the street. And of course they stopped.

If Pop can intercede for little ones from heaven, and faith tells us he can, then that's just the sort of miracle he'd win for them—miracles delivered in the silent language of love. That's true for us not-so-little ones, too.

As for me, I know I'll spend the rest of my life straining to hear that silent language and striving to speak it as Pop did.

TWENTY-SEVEN

I Confess

A Catholic shows his gray hairs when he says he can remember standing in line to go to confession. Just wait a bit, and you'll probably hear him segue to a consideration of the relative strengths of Willie Mays and Mickey Mantle. Or he may claim that he was at Woodstock.

I cannot hide my gray. I cast my baseball cap to the wind as I admit to you that I spent hours of my otherwise wasted youth standing in line at the confessional. At my school it was mandatory and thus, critics claim, "routine."

I'll grant the critics their point. For many of us, perhaps most of us, it *was* routine. One of my best buddies used to chatter all the time he was in line, saying he needed no time for reflection. Every week he confessed what he called the "standard sins." I can't recall that I was any more reflective than he was.

But I've come to believe that we Catholics were better off then, with our routine confessions, than we are today, with our save-it-for-the-deathbed attitude.

First off, there's something to be said for routine. Brushing my teeth, changing the oil in the car and mowing the lawn are three routines I'm not likely to give up as "meaningless" — though, I confess, I do them all in a distracted and unreflective way. The things in our lives that require regular maintenance *do* demand routines.

Next, we have to make allowance for grace. There are only two sacraments we can celebrate frequently, and confession is one of them. Sacraments are God's ordinary channels of grace, and we can't hope for anything extraordinary if we're not even taking him up on his ordinary means. No doubt God rewards our faithfulness to our routines, especially our sacramental routines, and especially when we don't feel like fulfilling them.

Last, but perhaps most importantly, I think all the great modern popes and saints and sages are right to decry our loss of the sense of sin. Most of us cluck-cluck along with them and imagine the Big Sins that go on in our world: drive-by shootings, drug wars, abortion and euthanasia. But I don't think that's what the great souls mean when they talk about the loss of the sense of sin. Or at least I don't think that's all they mean or even primarily what they mean.

The sad truth is that you and I are sinners. "If we say we have no sin, we deceive ourselves, and the truth is not in us" (1 John 1:8). Proverbs 24:16 speaks of "the righteous man" who "falls seven times"; I don't want to think about the number of times the rest of us fall.

But I have to think about it, because confession awaits. I confess that I do it routinely, though these days I try to do it reflectively as well.

In fact, several years ago we started going to confession as a family. Father keeps an Aquilina block in his schedule on a certain Tuesday of the month, and then we make our individual confessions privately, of course. We've seen many benefits to this approach.

First, it acknowledges that sin is a fact of our family life but also that forgiveness is its ordinary remedy.

Second, it eases the kids into the practice. At about three

years old the little ones start to insist on having their own time in the confession box. Father doesn't hear their confessions, but he does ask them questions about their prayer, and he usually asks them to work on some little virtue or good deed. One of his favorites seems to be "Hug your mom a lot"; we can tell almost as soon as we leave the church and the hugging begins.

What the kids are getting is elementary spiritual direction, and it's a great gift not only to them but to the parents who must share their residence. When it comes time for them to make their first sacramental confession, grace builds upon nature. It's an easy transition, with no fear at all and an absolution at the end.

Last but not least, the family practice establishes confession as a habit, something you do, like bathing, whether you feel like doing it or not. It's almost impossible for us to stay regular in confession unless we make it a habit, set an appointment and make it a fixed time every month, every other week, every week or however often we think best. The saints recommend weekly but lay down monthly as a minimum. The church requires us to go just once a year, but most of us need a little more than that.

At least I do. Just ask my wife!

TWENTY-EIGHT

Body Language

One of my favorite family photos is of my two oldest daughters, then aged five and three, sitting at the screen door watching our ninety-year-old neighbor Ed on his rider mower. That single snapshot tells many stories.

First it tells of my daughters' love for Ed, who called them "his girls" and carried lollipops along whenever he thought he might see them. When they heard the putt-putt of the mower, Mary Agnes and Rosemary rushed to their station at the door, and they stayed there until Ed had run his course over our entire lawn.

The picture's worth at least a thousand words about Ed's indomitability. At ninety years old he was mowing the rather large lawn of a perfectly capable thirty-something guy. "My lawn's too small," he'd say when I protested. "I hardly get the thing warmed up before I've finished the whole yard."

My own theory was that it galled him to have me shovel his walk during the winter. He'd much rather have done it himself, but some things were a little beyond his power. So in the summer he made up for it by mowing my lawn.

One day Mary Agnes asked me—out of nowhere—if I thought Ed was going to die. I said I supposed he would sometime, though at the moment he seemed as fit as any of us. Long retired from newspaper work, he still helped out at the hardware store every day. And his garden filled the salad bowls of families up and down the block.

A week after my conversation with Mary Agnes, Ed died suddenly and peacefully, while sitting in his favorite chair. None of us could quite imagine the neighborhood without his thousand kindnesses every week. None of us could imagine the disappearance of his omnipresent smile, punctuated by a stout cigar.

Through the many decades he lived on our block, Ed's day-to-day love was made flesh in work and gifts and timely words. "Sacrifices and offerings you have not desired, / but a body have you prepared for me" (Hebrews 10:5). God made the human body to speak a language of love, a language that Ed spoke fluently, in his every labor and in his lollipops.

Years later Mary Agnes and Rosemary and I still cannot imagine a world without Ed's smile or his work-worn hands, because his death *should not be*. It *must not be*. The world itself was not meant to outlive Ed's body and soul.

This, after all, is the creed we recite on Sunday morning: We believe in the resurrection of the body and life everlasting. Amen!

TWENTY-NINE

In the Public Square

A friend and I were grousing over coffee. He's a newspaper editor, and I was complaining about how Christian perspectives are woefully underrepresented in the media. He shot back that too few Christians take the time to write letters to the editor. I observed that editors of his ilk probably scare them away. So went the blame cycle for a few turns before we wisely turned the conversation to college football.

I walked away, though, with the lingering worry that we Christians have been removing ourselves from the public square. It's easy to see why. Ours is a society that even an optimistic pope—a man whose watchword was "Be not afraid"—described as a "culture of death." And that culture takes its formation from the media: TV, movies, the papers, the Web. Most of us, perhaps, would rather skip the morning paper than deal with the residual annoyance after reading it.

Yet if Christians opt out of the popular media entirely, who will reach the unchurched, and how? Whose voices will prevail on the letters page? We need to raise our voices. Editors and readers might meet us with a shrug or an insult, as some of Saint Paul's listeners in Athens met his teaching (see Acts 17:32), but we at least need to make the effort. God did not call us to be successful. He commanded us to tell the Good News to "all the world" (Mark 16:15).

We can make a difference. Even if we lack eloquence or

advanced degrees, we can help people see matters from another perspective.

Many years ago I was walking through downtown Pittsburgh with my son Michael, then four years old, and we passed a pro-life picket at an abortion mill. Michael asked what this was all about, and I explained that some doctors work to hurt babies, and these picketers were asking those doctors to stop. Michael was horrified; abortion went against everything he'd believed about doctors, who were, after all, supposed to help kids. He said he wanted to make a TV show that would help doctors to like babies.

About a week later he saw on TV a pro-life ad campaign that perfectly fit the bill. He was so excited that he wrote a short letter to the producers of the ad (I helped with the spelling): "I am four years old. I wanted to make a TV show so people would like babies. I'm glad you did." It was no deep philosophical statement, but the pro-life folks put it in their newsletter.

And then a very strange thing happened. Somehow a copy of their newsletter ended up in the hands of a pro-choice journalist at a nearby newspaper. Miraculously, the woman didn't pitch the paper in her wastebasket unread. In fact, her eyes fell on Michael's letter, and in her next newspaper column, she announced that she'd been converted!

I'm not making this up.

"Never before," she wrote, "have I looked at this issue from the point of view of a four-year-old child. I have always been an advocate of choice.... But now I feel like a hypocrite."[1]

Her column ran shortly before election day, 1994, in the Lewisburg, Pennsylvania, *Daily Journal*. Maybe she, in turn, changed the mind of a reader or two—or many.

If a kid can start that much in motion, imagine what you and I can do, if only we take the time to speak up in the public square.

THIRTY

The Truth About Butterfly Princess

My second youngest daughter is Isabella Maria, but she sings under the name Butterfly Princess. (I have no idea where she got the name.) She is quite famous in our home for the ballads she improvises. Her brother was so impressed that, when he could control his laughter well enough, he recorded instrumental backgrounds for them and produced a CD. The big hit was titled "I Love You (I'm Not Going to Kill You)."

Long before she was famous, Princess Isabella was keenly aware of her star status. It might have had something to do with her entourage of fawning older siblings. I used to think that a condescending attitude was an acquired trait, but Bella was condescending long before she could talk.

Like so many child stars, Bella is intelligent, articulate and frank. Once she came up to me as I was reading and began, unbidden, to report in the most affectionate tones a catalog of my physical flaws, beginning with blemishes on my skin. At the end, perhaps fearing that I might be offended, she added, "That's OK, though. I'll bet you were really handsome back when Mommy married you."

Well, they say that monks used to keep human skulls on their nightstands to remind them of how little they should value their own flesh. But I don't need any skull; I have the

Butterfly Princess to remind me of my shortcomings. Maybe when she grows a bit more in the spiritual life, she'll be able to identify my progress or regress in the ways of virtue.

Spiritual writers exhort us to be kind and honest critics with one another. In the old manuals this was called "fraternal correction," because it assumed a sibling (in Latin, *frater*) relationship between Christians. Jesus himself gave us the instruction: "If your brother sins against you, go and tell him his fault, between you and him alone. If he listens to you, you have gained your brother" (Matthew 18:15).

The problem is that most of us are proud, and we're often pretty thin-skinned. We would really rather hold on to our delusions of grandeur or, in my case, adequacy. So when Bella comes along, like Don Quixote's knightly nemesis, to hold up a mirror of unadorned truth, people like me can get irritated and even a little angry.

Isabella's frankness has its rough edges, and that's why we're all pitching in to help her learn diplomacy. We don't want her to be a constant object of the fury of the vain. There is, moreover, that fine line between frankness and rudeness, and my little princess should learn not to cross it if she ever hopes to be gainfully employed. Even pop divas can go much further in life if they're diplomatic with their inferiors.

Yet we also need to be careful not to discourage her from speaking the things we really need to hear but everyone else is too timid to say. Truth-tellers like Bella are a rare breed of butterfly, and they need to be protected and preserved.

Christian diplomacy is essential to healthy family life, and it is most certainly *not* a matter of sugarcoating bitter realities. If our family members don't teach us the lessons we need to learn, those lessons will come in a much more painful way, in the school of hard knocks.

So last night I pulled down our dusty 1911 *Catholic Encyclopedia* to get the guidelines for fraternal correction, and now I share them with you (translated into the terms of modern family life). The old masters tell us we have a duty to speak up when:

1. the fault to be corrected is a serious one;
2. there is no good reason to believe the offender will correct it without admonition;
3. there's reason to believe the correction will be heeded;
4. there's no one better to do the job;
5. the correction is unlikely to blow up in the reformer's face.

They say too that the person making the correction should pray for the one corrected, both before the admonition and afterward.

It sounds like a good family plan for peace and growth, once it becomes a habit. It makes for a household where everyone can sing "I Love You (I'm Not Going to Kill You)" and mean it.

THIRTY-ONE

Imagine the Possibilities

We began to notice the familiar signs and portents: Terri's strong cravings and even stronger aversions. But we knew for sure that Terri was pregnant when she bolted from the room in the middle of leading our family Bible study. Granted, the story of Joseph's reunion with his brothers is an emotional and moving narrative, but it's never inspired *me* to take such urgent action.

A new era began in our household as we anticipated our fifth delivery in the year 2000. My wife quite literally embodied the change. But something analogous to her bodily transformation took place in my own mind and heart. For now, the experts kept reminding us, Terri had reached AMA, "advanced maternal age." Now the risks were higher. Now more tests were in order.

I grew more protective of Terri. I worried when she drove at night. I bought a cell phone after years of resisting the trend. And if the kids showed their mother even the slightest disrespect, I felt an unfamiliar rage well up in my belly. All my being seemed redirected toward care and provision for Terri and the tiny baby on the way.

This is expectant fatherhood at APA, advanced paternal age. One moment I'd be exhilarated by the possibilities: a new life, a new person, a new personality in the wild mix we call our home. The next moment I'd be struck with certain fear:

another body and soul for whom I'm responsible, from now until eternity.

It can be scary. Each new life holds a seemingly infinite capacity for joy, accomplishment and grace, yet that same life also seems infinitely susceptible to suffering, failure and sin. And a father will share in each and all of those glories and heartaches, at least until death takes him away.

These glories and heartaches start early on. "I feel a kick!" and the whole family thrills to see little knees and elbows suddenly displace the skin on Mom's belly. A week later Mom and Dad might be huddling alone to pray about some unexpected bleeding. I've known the pride of watching my tiny baby move on a sonogram screen, and I've also known the agony of searching the same screen in vain, scanning desperately for the slightest hint of movement. We lost our second- and sixth-conceived children to miscarriage.

Of course, none of this is new to the world. I find Scripture tracking both my thrills and my terrors. "And a great sign appeared in heaven, a woman...with child and she cried out in her pangs of birth, in anguish for delivery. And another sign appeared in heaven; behold, a great red dragon...stood before the woman...that he might devour her child" (Revelation 12:1-4). Scholars say that, in one sense, this passage refers to Mary in Bethlehem, about to deliver the Savior, while Herod plotted the child's demise. In another sense the Christmas story, with all its promise and foreboding, is true in the life of every soul—yours and mine and all my children's.

"O little town of Bethlehem,...the hopes and fears of all the years are met in thee tonight."

THIRTY-TWO

About Nothing

A former colleague of mine, a Conservative Jew, used to tell this story.

The rabbi and the cantor were preparing the synagogue for the holy days. After setting down the books of the Law, the rabbi was so overwhelmed with emotion that he fell to the ground, repeating, "I am nothing, I am nothing."

The cantor, upon seeing his rabbi so humbled, dropped to the floor also and repeated after the rabbi, "I am nothing, I am nothing."

The two men lay prostrate for a long time, acknowledging their nothingness before God. Then a frail voice came from behind them. The cantor lifted his head to see the synagogue's janitor, a wisp of a man in his late seventies, lying prostrate and sobbing, "I am nothing, I am nothing."

The cantor turned to the rabbi and said, "So get a load of the janitor who thinks he can be nothing."

Humility is an elusive virtue. The more we pursue it—and the more we *seem* to acquire it—the more we take pride in our accomplishment, and we find ourselves back at square one. My friend John used to get laughs by saying he'd just finished his first book, *Humility and How I Achieved It.* The irony of the title reflects a paradox in our spiritual lives: We must pursue humility, yet the pursuit itself seems counter-productive.

What is humility?

There are many wrong ideas about it. Humility is not a cringing feeling of inferiority. It's not a constant state of abusive self-accusation or a vehement denial of every compliment. It has nothing to do with remaining an underachiever just so we can keep a low profile.

The philosopher Joseph Pieper defined it as man's estimation of himself *according to the truth*. Humility is seeing ourselves clearly as we are. We are made of mud, says the Book of Genesis, but we are made in the image and likeness of God (see Genesis 1:26-27; 2:7). Sometimes we're nearsighted and can see the mud but not the image of God. Other times we're farsighted, eager to own up to the godly part, yet we can't quite see the mud of which we're made. Either way we're not seeing ourselves as we should. Either way we're failing to be humble.

To be humble has something to do with self-esteem because it means to "estimate" ourselves most truly. That can make us uncomfortable. We like to think we're the face we put on for our friends, our Internet chat room or our coworkers. And it kills us when our wife or children point out our defects. We try to cover them over with excuses, but these just obscure the truth and blur our ability to see ourselves as we are.

Humility is necessary but elusive. What then should we do?

The saints give us good advice. They tell us to pursue a roundabout course.

First, always be grateful—to God, to friends, to enemies, to the kids, to your spouse. Get into the habit of saying "thank you" many times a day. If you're always grateful—even for insults and injustices—you'll always be humble.

Next, make a daily examination of conscience. And dig deep. Take what you dig up, regularly, to confession. Always start with the sin you're most ashamed of.

Then, always cultivate frankness in your family. Don't punish your spouse's honest criticism with pouting. Don't accuse your children of disrespect just because they dare to correct you when they sincerely think you are wrong.

Finally, pray. It's only in the presence of God that we can *sincerely* say that we are nothing, we are nothing.

THIRTY-THREE

War Games

I dropped off my son at his Scout patrol meeting, and I had about an hour to waste till it was time to pick him up. So I drove down the street and pulled into the shady section of the parking lot of the town library. It was a prefect summer evening. I rolled down the windows to enjoy the breeze, and I kicked back with a book.

I tend to be a rapt reader. I might raise my eyes for a locomotive if it brushes too close but little else. On this night I could only hear the near voices of small children.

Something made me look up, and I saw kids—six of them, maybe eight or nine years old—driving a lone boy down the street with their taunts. The boy broke into a jog for about twenty yards before sitting down on a park bench. I could see that he wasn't afraid; he was no longer running. But he was hurting.

A couple of the other kids shouted after him, but the rest clearly had lost interest. They turned down a side road and disappeared. When I looked again at the park bench, the boy was gone.

And so was any possibility of my reading. The locomotive had brushed close, for less than a minute's time, pulling freight from my own childhood. I couldn't go back to the novel on my lap.

To disbelieve in the devil or in the immense human capacity for sin, an adult must carry on some mighty self-deception.

First he must forget any moment from his childhood when he was the object of cruelty. Then he must forget all the moments when he perpetrated cruelty—on his friends, his enemies, his siblings or the kids on the block who just "didn't matter." Once he has done that, he can fool himself into believing that he's a fine fellow, safe from evil's sway.

But the cruelty we learn as children—as its victims or as its perpetrators—remains hidden in an unexamined heart. We grow and take our place in the workforce, find a social set and join a prayer group. Yet we still find a thousand subtle ways to stick the knife in and twist it. "Boy, did I show her!" "You should have seen the look on his face!" "He'll learn never to mess with me again."

We justify ourselves as vindicators, champions of good who give the *real* evil people their comeuppance. But we differ from those kids in the library yard only in our degree of culpability. We, as mature Christians, should know better.

Where does all this begin? In the fire of hell or in the darkness of our own hearts?

I can't claim to know the proportion, in those children's actions or in my own—from my childhood and from some all-too-recent days of my adulthood. What I do know is that, from its very early days, this life is warfare, spiritual warfare, and it's imperative that we see the battlefield clearly. Sometimes our battle is to speak up in defense of the neighborhood's victims. Sometimes we must struggle mightily not to say the words that are rushing to our lips and not to return cruelty in kind.

It's never too early to train our children in the weapons of this war: prayer, Scripture, trust in the Lord. That training is something neither they nor we will ever outgrow. We can fight with confidence if we know God and know ourselves. We can win the spiritual war if we're constant in the skirmishes and call on the name of the Lord. Let's keep each other in prayer.

THIRTY-FOUR

Telling Beads

The cabbie nodded when I told him my destination, a suburb far distant from the airport. As I ducked into the back seat, he picked up his radio transmitter and reported to his dispatcher in a language I couldn't identify. Assuming he spoke no English, I settled in for a long, quiet ride.

When I'm away on business, I like to pray for Terri and the kids. I took out my rosary and began to move silently along the beads.

The cabbie continued his radio conversation as we wound our way through the airport exits. I assumed he was getting directions to my hotel. He turned to me and asked, with a perfect British accent, "May I borrow your pen, please?"

Taken by surprise, I reached into my pocket with my rosary hand and gave him what he needed. "Thank you," he said and went back to his rapid-fire exchange with the dispatcher, which ended in a litany of route numbers.

"Thank you," he said again as he handed my pen back to me. Then we sat in silence for a few miles of high-speed straight-away on a wide-open interstate.

The cabbie was the one to break the silence. "I saw your beads," he said. "Are you Muslim?"

His eyes intent on the road ahead, he couldn't see my eyebrows arch upward. I replied in an even tone, "No, Christian."

He held up his right hand so I could see the string of

wooden beads he kept by the steering wheel of the cab. "I am Muslim," he said. "I pray my beads all day long."

I wasn't sure what to say, so we sat silently for a bit. Then he asked, "May I be frank with you?"

"Sure," I said, bracing myself for I didn't know what.

"You are the first American I've seen praying. In my country people pray all the time, everywhere."

I asked him where he was from, and he told me. "It is what you might call a repressive place," he said. "The law is very severe. But I will go back there at the end of the year, because I cannot raise a family in your land."

He broke off suddenly and then added, "I am sorry. I do not mean to offend you. But all week long I take men to places where they work hard and for what? So that on weekends I can take them to places where they behave like animals."

He went on to describe nights that were pageants of drunkenness, promiscuity and violence—public and shameless acts for which a man or woman could be executed in his faraway country. "When men cease to live in the presence of God," he said, "they begin to live as animals."

I sat in stunned silence. He had said it all. But perhaps he felt he had gone too far. With a cabbie's skill he steered the conversation down easier streets, asking about my plans for the weekend. I assured him that my nights would be quite tame.

I have spent my days since—thanks to that cabbie—in the presence of God as perhaps I had never before.

"The Catholic Church," says the *Catechism*, "recognizes in other religions that search, among shadows and images, for the God who is unknown yet near since he gives life and breath and all things and wants all men to be saved. Thus, the Church considers all goodness and truth found in these religions as 'a preparation for the Gospel and given by him who enlightens all men that they may at length have life'" (*CCC*, 843).[1]

I pray that my cabbie is happy with his family, wherever he lives today, and that he finds the true Light of the World, Jesus Christ. I am grateful for the encouragement he gave me, perhaps unwittingly, to be a fitting witness to that Light.

THIRTY-FIVE

Immortality

"What does she see in him?"

How many times have you heard that line? How often have you spoken it? Love is, for the most part, a mystery knowable only by the lover and the loved. And even then...

I imagine that almost twenty-five years ago, as I picked Terri up for our first date, her neighbors on the dorm floor must have asked The Question. I imagine that throughout the next two years they repeated it at least as often as I did. I still don't know what she sees in me. Yet here she is, at this late hour, nursing our sixth child, Teresa Carmella. God is good.

His love, too, is an unfathomable mystery. I know my own sins: the grudges and vanities, laziness and ill will, I harbor in my heart. All of these are abuses committed against him above all. Yet he would take on flesh for my sake! Like a man crazy with love, he allowed himself to look ridiculous before crowds and endured pain and even death, just so that he could spend eternity by my side. What does he see in me?

So perhaps love is a mystery to all but the lover. We the beloved can only wonder why.

Throughout Holy Week and the Triduum, such wonder can be spectacular if we give ourselves over to earnest prayer. "What does he see in me?" can be a frightful question when we consider the state of our souls, our need for his mercy. But this in itself is a gift preparing us for love by inspiring us to repentance, gratitude and, at last, joy.

Saint Augustine taught that man's deepest desire is to look upon one who looks back in love. My wife looks at little Teresa and sometimes glances my way. So Terri and I both looked upon the purity of the Host throughout the loving vigil of Holy Thursday.

Our desire is to live and to live more abundantly. This desire for immortality draws a man and woman together in love. And in a purely natural sense, their love grants them immortality in the children who survive them. The great philosopher of medicine Herbert Ratner once told me: "Go back to Aristotle. Every living thing tries to be immortal and divine. They can't do it by the continuation of bodily life; their bodies are mortal. So they reproduce themselves. The drive is so powerful in nature to keep living things going."

And Jesus' love is all the stronger—stronger even than death—coming to us now with promises of immortality in body and soul, everlasting life. "I will raise him up at the last day" (John 6:40).

"I believe in the resurrection of the body." This Easter Vigil I sang my love in the Mass as I held Teresa Carmella, sleeping close to my heart. And I knew that my Redeemer lives—though I still don't know what he sees in me.

THIRTY-SIX

A Letter on Birth Control

Dear Frank,

Thank you for taking time to reply, at such great length, to my article about contraception. I'll try to respond to your concerns as best I can.

Since you didn't cite sources, I can't check your quotations in their original context. I'll assume, however, that they are all accurate representations of the saints' intentions. I can sum them up thus: Some saints were very wrong about sex.

This is not news. Give me a day and I can come up with even more disturbing quotes from the saints and popes—not only on matters sexual but also on war, tolerance, torture and so on. Saints have been wrong on occasional points of doctrine. This should make us humble. You and I too might be wrong now and then.

History should make us even more humble and less eager to take up a practice that's suddenly commonplace after two millennia of universal Christian condemnation. Since you say you've spent thirty years studying the issue of contraception, I won't bore you by rehashing the condemnations made by Martin Luther, John Calvin and John Wesley, not to mention Mohandas Gandhi and George Orwell. Nor will I discuss the witness of good Christian families of all those many years.

But since you've used your family as an example, I beg your patience while I use mine. I am the seventh child of my parents; both were forty-seven when I was born. My father painted heavy machinery for a living. By most of today's material standards, we lived in poverty. My two brothers and I shared one large bed; my sisters shared another. Like you, my father spent some time in the Navy early in his marriage. In the recession of the late 1940s, Pop went without regular work for more than a year.

My parents surely knew hardship, but they knew it as God's will, and I never realized we were "poor" till I left home. My parents' home was the happiest home I've ever seen. It was a haven for neighbors and relatives who needed a place to turn for help, to cry or to hide from abuse. It was no different as my parents approached their eighty-fifth birthdays. Mom and Pop continued to enjoy a warm, respectful, affectionate relationship.

My wife and I wish no less for our children and us. We've been married for twenty-one years. About fifteen years ago Terri entered the Catholic church. The consistency of church doctrine on human love was a key reason for her intellectual conversion; the witness of many happy, noncontracepting families was another inspiration to her. We try our best to live this unified life of Catholic teaching. So far it's brought us great joy, with six beautiful children. No guilt-wracked confessions to speak of, no neuroses about sex.

I acknowledge that my acceptance of this teaching is perhaps extraordinary in our country and in our time. And I thank God for his mercies. Tragically, half of American Catholic marriages today break up. For couples who follow church teaching on birth control, however, the figure is far less, perhaps one-twentieth.

Let's look a little more closely at America's high divorce rate in these years of widespread contraception. I agree with you that a majority act with sound reasons and in good faith. I'm all for the *sensus fidelium* (sense of the faithful). But can we call couples "faithful" who are not even faithful to each other—who indeed are divorcing at such an alarming rate?

You seem to reduce the sense of the faithful to Gallup Poll results. This neglects the communion of saints and what Chesterton called "the democracy of the dead,"[1] the notion that so many good people from so many generations just might have some wisdom to offer us, even in our enlightened times. Your model sets any Christian teaching on shaky ground. I'm sure you've seen the polls that show that 70 percent of American Catholics do not believe in the real presence of Christ in the Eucharist. Should we take this, too, as gospel?

According to your notions of authority, this is all we're left with. In your letter you dismiss papal pronouncements, council documents and tradition. Implicitly you reject the clear teaching of the Second Vatican Council, Popes Pius XI, Pius XII, John XXIII, Paul VI, John Paul II and Benedict XVI, as well as the *Catechism of the Catholic Church*. You've pretty much poisoned all the wells of authority but the Gallup Poll, and you declare that one infallible.

You explicitly reject the Council of Trent teaching on celibacy. But judging only by your snippet, I must say that Trent seems no more "unhealthy" than Jesus and Saint Paul on the same subject. The only healthy view of celibacy, as I understand it, is that it is a call to give up something very good for something even better (see *CCC*, 1620).

As a married man, I feel not a bit diminished by this. I don't need a clerical collar to gain perfect holiness or human dignity. Going back to the New Testament, I see Jesus and Saint Paul, both celibates, exalting my vocation to marriage, even as they exalt their own call a little bit more (see Matthew 19:12; 1 Corinthians 7).

Your other reference from Trent seems fine to me too. It's reasonable for Christians to say no to sex that is motivated only by sensuality and pleasure. To do otherwise is to reduce our spouses to mere objects, instruments for our gratification. Sex is much better than that.

Sex, I would say, is better than most people know. You say, and I agree, that most people don't understand the difference between natural and artificial methods of birth control. The fact is that they haven't been taught this difference. But it's simply the difference between trying to work with nature and trying to reengineer nature. The difference between Natural Family Planning (NFP) and contraception is the difference between dieting (or fasting) and binge-purge bulimia. Just as a bulimic person wants the pleasures of food without the weight gain, a contraceptive couple wants the pleasures of sex without one of the proper and natural ends of sex.

So who's healthy here? Just as intelligent dieting shows a healthier attitude toward food than does bulimia, I think that the church checks out healthy on sex.

You really should give *Humanae Vitae* a close reading or at least a fairer treatment than you did in your letter. When you say that the difference in the means of controlling fertility "is a difference without a moral distinction," you assume what you ought to prove. It seems to me that much of the encyclical is devoted to making just that distinction.

Finally, I have to take issue with your claim that contraceptive use "reduces abortion." This is simply untrue. Planned Parenthood's own studies have shown that when a country accepts contraception, abortion soon follows, and an increase in abortions tends to follow an increase in contraceptive use. And I assume you know that the pill itself, in most of its forms, is abortifacient. An attorney used this fact in arguing the pro-abortion position before the U.S. Supreme Court some years back.

You were kind to write, Frank. I read your letter and reflected on it. I'd encountered most of the ideas before, but having to respond made me stronger in my convictions. I stand by all I wrote.

Let's keep each other in prayer.

THIRTY-SEVEN

Lives of the Saints

M y grandfather, Calogero Aquilina, never smiles at me. He gazes with only the most solemn of expressions. Such was the portrait style of the 1920s, when he died a young man.

Yet I know he looks on me with love. For I am the son of his son, Mike, whom Calogero loved with constancy.

My dad remembered trailing his papa everywhere. He would tag along to work—Calogero was a public school janitor—and shoot baskets while his father mopped the court. Because Calogero could read and write both English and Italian, my father often accompanied him when he helped other Sicilian immigrants write letters home, settle citizenship issues or obtain proper working papers.

My father was ten years old when his father was taken to a special hospital for tuberculosis patients, a place the little boy visited only once. Ever afterward he recalled that the rooms were huge, and everything there was pure white—the walls, the furniture and the medical equipment.

Calogero's obituary occupied almost an entire broadsheet page in the Italian newspaper of Scranton, Pennsylvania, and his photograph was prominent, a journalistic rarity in 1926. This good janitor's death was *news* to the people. The long columns describe his funeral procession of seventy-three cars—five of them holding only flowers—and more than a thousand people. (I was surprised to learn that there were seventy-three cars in my little town in 1926.) Police stopped traffic along the route from St. Rocco's Church to St. John's Cemetery.

I only recently uncovered the obituary, though I knew my grandfather from my father's stories. Till I saw the details in black and white, part of me had dismissed Pop's heroic descriptions as affectionate exaggeration. Now, however, I know it's all true: Calogero's works of mercy, his self-sacrifice and his sense of family and community.

And I know that these deeds and these qualities did not die; they lived on in his children, my father and his six siblings. I am witness to that. And the virtues remain with Calogero himself, like a fine linen garment (see Revelation 19:8).

The early Christians saw this reality much more clearly than we do: heaven is real; purgatory is real; and our dear ones, the holy souls of our family and friends, remain near to us forever. More, they are nearer to God even as they seem farther from us, and they intercede for us.

I am learning to know the nearness of Calogero, the grandfather who never lived to carry me on his shoulder. He carries me now on some difficult days. This is my communion of saints. This is our communion of saints.

THIRTY-EIGHT

Just Say It!

Young married men do foolish things. They rush in impetuously, careless of the causal chain they're setting in motion, thoughtless about what their actions might mean for all the remaining decades of their lives.

I know I was that way. On Valentine's Day when we were newlyweds, I did something for which I've paid dearly in all the years since. I wrote a poem for Terri, a poem praising her as a summit peak of God's creation, and I put it in an envelope and gave it to her.

It was a bull's-eye. Tears welled in her eyes, and she hugged me and thanked me. I went off to work smiling, and I came home to find the poem framed and standing prominently on a mantle. In our little apartment, for days afterward, I was The Man, I knew it, and I was loving it. I could do no wrong.

Hey, I thought to myself, *this lady's no dope. She didn't marry an English major for nothing.* We had reached a new and higher plateau in marriage, I was sure, and all because of the Valentine's Day poem.

Months passed, and the poem remained there in its frame, to remind me daily of my literary prowess. Come January, though, I began to get other reminders, as Terri spoke of the framed edition as "last year's poem," which would surely pale before "*this* year's poem." In the presence of witnesses, she would praise "last year's poem" as she pointed out that Valentine's Day was just a month away.

Uh-oh. Immediately I beheld a vision of what I had done in that months-ago moment in light of all its lifelong effects: I had pledged myself to Valentine poems ever afterward, till death or a reasonable facsimile thereof.

The pressure was on. But English majors thrive under deadlines. I produced a second poem and renewed my status as hero, genius and litterateur.

I kind of grew to like the writing of love poems. In order to psych myself up for the following year, I would spend a couple of months reading the great poetry of the English language, and gradually I developed opinions about poetry. I found myself drawn into the debates going on just then about the "New Formalism," the return to rhyme and rhythm (meter) in poetry. I myself was partial to formal poems, and so I subscribed to the New Formalist journals. My favorite by far was *Plains Poetry Journal,* which was edited by a poet I greatly admired, Jane Greer.

One day, on a whim, I submitted one of my Valentine poems to *Plains,* and within a week I received word that it was accepted for publication. This, to me, was like having a portrait I painted of Terri placed in the National Gallery or the Louvre. I had hymned my wife's beauty, and now readers everywhere would be joining in the hymn.

I was once again The Man. The next issue carried the poem, "At the Corner of Business and Memory":

You are city traffic in my day;
my mind, you know, a one-way street.
At nine o'clock you're fifteen feet

through intersections, blocking way
for what I was about to say.

This boardroom needs a traffic cop
to press you on—"Let's move it, doll"—
to blow his whistle, waving all
my thoughts of business to the top
of midday hills. Again they stop

for flashing lights and tracks and trains
of thought. A siren blares and wanes.
Then, speeding cross the passing lanes
comes you! You wink at work, and then
it's back, sweet gridlock, once again.

OK, so it's not T.S. Eliot or Robert Frost, but T.S. Eliot and Robert Frost were never The Man in our little apartment, not even for a day, not even for an hour. Other journals took other poems in the following years.

Poetry is language at its most exalted, most refined and most powerful. It's the right language for human love. When we're young and infatuated, the words pour out of our hearts and onto the paper. As we grow older, busier and more distracted, sometimes it takes more work. And sometimes we just get writer's block.

One year I was stumped, and I was tempted to just write, "Roses are red, violets are blue," and so on, but a sudden inspiration came. I would write about writer's block. Terri (once again) loved it. This one was called "Be My Valentine Anyway":

Somewhere, a place I've never found,
roses, violets, quilt the ground.

Of course they're red, and yes, they're blue,
and each begins a poem for you.

These flowers bloom in bitter cold.
And men will pluck them (so I'm told)
and give them, with their trailing verses,
to secretaries, wives and nurses.

For miles round this garden, then,
rise poems from the lips of men,
poems that were meant for you,
of blossoms red and, oh, so blue,

and sugar sweet!
　　　But fate, but fate—
fate keeps me from the garden gate.
And I've no map, no poem, just this:
these sixteen lines, a prayer, a kiss.

That one never made it to *Plains Poetry Journal*, but it did the job at home for another year.

The winter my dad died, I was desolate and not at all in a poetic mood, but I wrote about what a consolation our marriage had been in those terrible, final months.

You could not stop the winter storm for me.
So you built a house and kept it warm for me.
You could not stop the world's alarms for me.
Instead you opened up your arms for me.
You could not keep my childhood here for me.
So you gave me children, drew them near for me.
Could heaven be more close than this for me?
God made your healing, saving kiss for me.

Terri wept and told me, "You didn't have to write anything." But I knew I did, if not for her sake then at least for mine. After more than a decade, the annual poem was a custom, a tradition. It was normal, and I needed to steer my life back to normal.

On a more recent Valentine's Day, I had to be away from home, and the high points of my days were the moments when Terri and I spoke on the phone. It was those moments that produced my poem for the year:

Some hundred miles of cable span the skies
And stretch beneath the streets from you to me.
Expensive men and instruments assize
Your signal strength and tone and clarity.

But where's the gauge to count or man to mark
The elements conveyed across the wire
Each time you call: the copper takes the spark
And bears your voice, your warmth, your light, your fire.

I readily admit that writing the Valentine poems, at my current stage of life, is work. But it's also a discipline, a guarantee that I'll say the things that should be said. Young lovers just blurt out whatever's on their mind or heart. We older lovers, well, we feel the feelings, but we're slower to say something crazy and foolish. We'd rather *do* something than say something.

Showing our love in deeds is a good thing, but we should not neglect the words. We may outgrow the urgent need to *speak* our minds and hearts, but we never outgrow the need to *hear* assurances of love and affirmations of beauty and goodness. We don't ache to say things as we once did, but we always ache to hear them.

I'm not advocating a worldwide wave of spousal poetry here, but I am making a plea for greater freedom of speech when it comes to expressions of affection. Our tendency is to make excuses, as Golde did in *Fiddler on the Roof.*

"I worked sixty hours this week to pay your bills. And I just mowed the lawn and trimmed the hedges. Isn't that love?" Well, yes, it is; but say it anyway.

"I feed your children three meals a day, don't I? And I keep the house from collapsing into chaos. Isn't that an expression of love?" Yes, but as we always tell our three-year-old, use words, please.

There are many things we'll regret saying over the course of a marriage, but "I love you" isn't one of them, and neither is "You're beautiful," or, "You're the best mom (or dad) I could have chosen for my children," or, "You're an excellent provider." These lines, once heard, are never forgotten; they're gifts guaranteed to last a lifetime. They exceed the greatest poetry in their power. And still they don't cost us a dime or even a modicum of effort.

If you need any more reason to put your love into words, ponder your God. He has always treated his relationship with humankind as more than a love affair. In both the Old Testament and the New, he speaks of it as a marriage. He loves us that much.

And he's certainly shown his love with deeds. No one has more of a right than the Almighty to say, "Look what I've done for you. Isn't that love?" He might have created the world out of nothing and left it at that. Creation, after all, is an act of love. He might have delivered us from slavery or brought us back from exile and gone on to the next task. But he didn't "just do it"; he said it, too. He did it all, and then he told us anyway, "I have loved you with an everlasting love" (Jeremiah 31:3). And he never tired of saying it. Indeed, he left us a Bible full of poetry, all about his love for us.

I'm grateful for that, and I tell him so. I'm no Saint John of the Cross, and I've never been able to carry off a love poem to our Lord. But as I grow older, my two great relationships—my marriage and my life in Christ—seem so close as to be inseparable.

More, more my world is here.
I wake, I work, I stay
where I can know you near.

Your curtains keep my day.
Your bed describes my night.
We sleep while angels pray

that I may never stray,
not far nor long from sight
of Love, by day, by night.

THIRTY-NINE

The Spousal Secret

I hate public speaking. It terrifies me to look out on a sea of faces or, worst of all, to look out and see only floodlights, knowing that behind that glare is a sea of faces, all looking at me and probably in a disapproving way—if they're awake.

It's something I have to get over, because God has made it clear to me that speaking is part of my vocation. But that struggle is not in my plans for the near term. Too many other vices and weaknesses are ahead of glossophobia in queue.

In the meantime I respond to speaking invitations with a form letter I call my "crucifix before the vampire" letter. It's supposed to drive away pastors and committees and conference organizers by making unreasonable demands of them. Most of the time it works.

Once, though, someone called with a plea. This was a friend, so I was already weakened: I couldn't send the form letter. He explained that he was in a jam, and he needed a speaker. I was so busy that I had no time to argue, so I hastily agreed and asked him to e-mail me the topic.

I was busy, so I didn't open the e-mail until shortly before I was supposed to give the talk.

When I did, my blood ran cold. I put my head on my desk and groaned before turning to my wife: "Can you give this talk instead of me?"

"What's it about?"

"It says:'The secret to being a good husband.'"

I was not encouraged to hear her laugh as hard as she did.

"Seriously, honey," I said, "you have to tell me what to say."

When she'd regained her composure and dried her eyes, she said, "Tell them the secret to being a good husband is...chocolate." And she left me alone with my frightening task.

I typed the word *chocolate* on the page but got no further. So I decided to procrastinate and read the newspaper online.

Now, this was, on the surface, a very bad idea, because for me the newspapers usually spell the death of inspiration and the beginning of aggravation. But this time was different. It must have been a slow news day, because on the *New York Times* Web site, I found a most remarkable feature.

Some clever writer had asked several famous scientists a leading question: "What do you believe is true even though you cannot prove it?" Many answers were interesting in a nerdy sort of way, but one was a keeper. It was from David Buss, a psychologist at the University of Texas. He said that, in spite of his utter lack of proof, he believed in "true love":

> I've spent two decades of my professional life studying human mating. In that time, I've documented phenomena ranging from what men and women desire in a mate to the most diabolical forms of sexual treachery. I've discovered the astonishingly creative ways in which men and women deceive and manipulate each other.... But throughout this exploration of the dark dimensions of human mating, I've remained unwavering in my belief in true love.[1]

As I read on, I was surprised and captivated by one phrase in particular, "profound self-sacrifice," which isn't in the ordinary lexicon of evolutionary psychology. Yet it rang true for me because it echoed Christian doctrine. It made sense in Dr. Buss's context as well. Profound self-sacrifice is indeed the thing that has to go beyond all barriers and boundaries, and it's most certainly something that will defy all scientific measurements.

Profound self-sacrifice—sustained over many years and many decades—is what sets true love apart from mere "mesmerizing attraction" and "the desire to combine DNA."

And, shameless exploiter that I am, it occurred to me immediately that my guardian angel was writing my good-husband talk for me. So I started typing with reckless abandon. No matter what my lovely wife may say, profound self-sacrifice trumps even *chocolate* on any list of the qualities of true love.

What's more, it's not just for husbands. Profound self-sacrifice is what being a good wife, being a good parent and being a good son or daughter are all about. So maybe the husbands who didn't want to change their lives would at least go home from my talk with advice they could preach at their wives.

Of course, I didn't need to learn marital self-sacrifice from the *New York Times*. It was waiting for me all along in the Bible: "Husbands, love your wives, as Christ loved the Church and gave himself up for her, that he might sanctify her" (Ephesians 5:25-26). But even the *Times* must occasionally serve God's providence.

Self-sacrifice means that, for the sake of our marriages, we have to give up more than our bad habits. We need to give up ourselves, our wants and our preferences, our pet peeves and even our perceived needs. We need to make sacrifice our second nature.

The self-sacrifice must take place in an almost literal way. On our wedding day we made the move from *I* to *we*. In marriage the *I* must be sacrificed. So everything—hobbies, fascinations, cars, career goals, the desire to spend an hour reading a book beside the fire—everything in life must take on a new value relative to the good of the spouse.

Such sacrifice comes naturally to young people. We see it in all the courtship customs of the world. Men stay up all night strumming a guitar in order to serenade their beloved. The patriarch Jacob tended the flocks of his future father-in-law for seven years, and then seven more, and never uttered a word of complaint. Love inspires sacrifice. A heart madly in love demands to give itself in sacrifice.

As we grow older in a relationship, we can settle back into seeking our own comfort rather than the good of our spouse. Yet we should not let the fire die. We need to rekindle it if we have let it die, and the only way to do that is to begin to make sacrifices.

Love calls for profound self-sacrifice worked out in small details. Sometimes this will require heroism. The newspapers like to run feel-good stories about spouses donating organs for one another, and my love and yours may require such extreme forms of heroism someday. But most of the time *profound* self-sacrifice is more low-key.

Sometimes we'll have to stay up all night with a crying baby and then get dressed and put on a happy face for work the next day. Sometimes the greatest sacrifice will be to change the diaper as soon as we're asked—or better, before anyone else has noticed that it needs changing. Sometimes the greatest sacrifice of all will be to arrive home at the end of the day wearing a smile—just because we know that a smile will make the house and the evening much brighter than the weary expression that more accurately reflects our day. We want our first thoughts to be for our spouse rather than for ourselves.

In marriage we should, as much as possible, sacrifice our desire to criticize, our urge to complain or whine. Here's a little trick I learned: if I feel the need to complain, I go to a quiet place and complain to the Blessed Virgin Mary. If I can look Mary in the eye (so to speak) and still bring myself to grumble about my wife, then maybe—just maybe—I have something legitimate to complain about. Most times, however, as soon as I approach that perfect wife and mother—and even before I begin to formulate my prayer—she shows me that the fault is mine and not Terri's.

On rare occasions, of course, I'm right in my grumbling. Even then I've found it a good policy to "complain" to Our Lady for at least two weeks before lodging the complaint with my wife. In the meantime Our Lady often will rush ahead and solve the problem for me, letting Terri know about it without my help. Other times Our Lady wins me the grace to live more patiently with the situation.

Jesus offered precious little in the way of practical advice for husbands and wives, but he did have something to say about friendship, and marriage is the deepest form of friendship. He told his apostles that there is no greater love than to lay down your life for a friend, and then he told them a curious thing: He said that they are his friends if they keep his commands (see John 15:13-14).

Many centuries ago Saint Ambrose puzzled over this line. It's not customary, he pointed out, for friends to go around giving orders to one another. So what could Jesus have meant?

Ambrose took from Jesus' statement that we should ask ourselves: What would my friend command if he or she had such authority over me? Translation for me: I should anticipate the needs of my wife and do what she wants me to do before she asks me to do it.

My desires might be very good and wholesome, but that is precisely the sort of thing that is good for the sort of worship we call "profound sacrifice." It goes without saying that we should give up immoral habits and bad things. But the Israelites offered cattle and sheep to God because they valued cattle and sheep. God is pleased especially when we voluntarily sacrifice good things for the sake of others, especially the other to whom we're married.

Marriage is a sacrament, and so in marriage we need to imitate Jesus in the sacrament of sacraments, the holy Eucharist. We need to give ourselves entirely, as he gives himself entirely. We need to live wholly for the sake of the other.

We don't need the *New York Times* to tell us what Saint Paul put to poetry so long ago: that true love is identical with profound self-sacrifice, and it is always the "more excellent way" (1 Corinthians 12:31).

FORTY

By Way of the Family

It's only right that, before we conclude a book on Catholic family life, we should bring it on home. Home in this case is heaven, our origin and goal. But heaven should be our homes as well, because if we do family life right, our families will become heaven's outposts on earth.

If that sounds impossible, you can be sure that it is for us mortals. But "with God nothing will be impossible" (Luke 1:37), and he wants our family's happiness much more than we do.

Think about what he's done to prove it: "For God so loved the world that he gave his only-begotten Son, that whoever believes in him should not perish but have eternal life. For God sent the Son into the world, not to condemn the world, but that the world might be saved through him" (John 3:16–17).

God so loved the world that he sent his only Son, and he sent him not just to crowds of people or nations or even congregations. He sent him, first of all, to you and to me; and our Father was thinking specifically of you and me when he sent Jesus, his Son, to be the Savior of the world.

We know from the Scriptures that God is always active in history. From the first pages of Genesis, he was preparing the way for the last pages of Revelation. In the Garden of Eden, he foretold the day when Jesus would arrive to save the world (see Genesis 3:15).

So when God broke into human history by his Incarnation, you can be sure that all the details of the story were important. In the details he's trying to tell us something. Here's one significant detail that merits our attention: when God sent us a Savior, he sent him by way of a family—the Holy Family of Nazareth.

God could have chosen another way. Jesus could have blazed to earth like some superhero from another planet or shown up a mysterious stranger. But the fact is that the Father entrusted his Son to human parents, Mary and Joseph.

What can we learn from the fact that Jesus had an earthly family? What does it mean for parents and children today? And is there anything about the Holy Family's home life that we can imitate?

The Hidden Life

An obvious way to approach these questions is to take a closer look at the family that Jesus grew up in. What was God's own family home like?

It's hard to say at first glance. Though two of the Gospels—Matthew and Luke—describe the events surrounding Jesus' birth, Scripture offers only one anecdote about his childhood: the family pilgrimage to the Jerusalem temple (see Luke 2:41–52).

Some early Christians were frustrated by Scripture's lack of detail and tried to fill in the blanks by inventing spectacular stories. In one collection, the so-called *Infancy Gospel of Thomas*, Jesus breathes life into toys in order to outdo his friends; he stretches beams in his father's carpentry shop when the wood comes up short; he strikes dead a teacher who dares to punish him. And when the neighbors complain, Saint Joseph directs

Mary to not let this fictitious Jesus outside the door, "because anyone who angers him dies." (In another of these sensational writings, cruel playmates are turned into goats!)

There are good reasons why we don't find such stories in the Bible. The church rejected them as untrue, and indeed they don't meet the standard of miracles set in the real Gospels. "Superboy of Nazareth" works wonders to exact revenge, gain professional advantage and ward off those who attack or insult him. None of this jibes with the Jesus we know, who worked miracles in order to serve others and who patiently endured insults and even violence from those who opposed him.

We can be fairly certain that Jesus spent his childhood doing nothing spectacular. In fact, John tells us that he performed his first miracle when he changed water into wine at Cana (see John 2:1-11). Apparently the glory of God's only Son was hidden for the first three decades of his earthly life. For this reason Jesus' growing-up years are often referred to as the "hidden life" in Nazareth.

So our question remains: what can we learn from the fact that God entered history by way of the family? Surely we are called in some way to imitate the Holy Family. But how can we ever learn from what we cannot begin to see?

Fortunately we *can* begin to catch glimpses into the "hidden life" as we reflect a bit more on the evidence from Scripture. The *Catechism* sums it up like this: "During the greater part of his life Jesus shared the condition of the vast majority of human beings: a daily life spent without evident greatness, a life of manual labor. His religious life was that of a Jew obedient to the law of God, a life in the community" (*CCC*, 531). This gives us much to think about.

Our Model for Family Life

Most obviously, the Holy Family had a deep spiritual life. As they raised Jesus, both Mary and Joseph set an example of prayer and trust in God. Each had heard and accepted God's plan through the message of an angel; they were obedient and attuned to the Holy Spirit.

They were steeped in Scripture too. Mary's prayer, the Magnificat, is rich in Old Testament quotations (see Luke 1:46-55). Joseph also must have known his Scripture: Jewish fathers of his day had the main responsibility for instructing sons about God's revelation to Israel.

From Jesus' adulthood we can glimpse the prayer life he learned from his parents. He prayed the morning offering of pious Jews (see Mark 12:29-30). He prayed spontaneously and with his friends. He fasted and marked holy days, traveling to Jerusalem to observe the Passover and other pilgrimage festivals of the Jewish year. All these habits he probably acquired from his home life in Nazareth.

Work, too, was important to Jesus' family. Joseph, as the family breadwinner, was skilled in a trade that he passed along to Jesus. In adulthood Jesus was called not just "Joseph's son" but "the carpenter's son" (Luke 4:22; Matthew 13:55). The image of Joseph and Jesus working side by side in the workshop and on construction projects makes a statement about the essential dignity of work. It also suggests that they knew something about realities like on-the-job fatigue, fussy customers and late payments!

It is a safe bet that the Holy Family's lifestyle was very simple. Mary and Joseph were poor (recall the description of Jesus' birth and presentation in Luke 2:1-24). It is likely that from Mary's example in the frugal keeping of house Jesus drew many of his favorite stories: a woman finding just the right cloth to patch a piece of clothing, a woman setting aside leaven for the next day of baking, a widow searching her house for a lost coin.

Hard work, struggling to meet the bills, taking long road trips, prayer and simple devotions: this is what the real Gospels tell us about the Holy Family. It's a far cry from the divine Dennis the Menace who drives his parents crazy by turning people into goats!

It's so…ordinary. And in a way, isn't that what makes it scary? Those long-ago yarn-spinners preferred to emphasize how different the Holy Family was. This lets us off the hook. Who could blame us for not imitating them? After all, it's not as if we come home to find our kids breathing life into Winnie the Pooh or Barbie!

If the Holy Family were so different from us, we'd be free of our obligation to imitate them. But Scripture and the *Catechism* point to our duty to make our homes holy as theirs was holy.

God entered history through a family in order to make family life holy and show us how to live in our homes. The hard work, the piety, the obedience, the active seeking for God's will—all these are virtues *we* can imitate at home.

Trinitarian Life

There's a still more profound reason why God entered history through a family. Pope John Paul II spoke of this in his Letter to Families, issued in 1994. The family, he suggested, is where God the Son has always been at home, from all eternity, because the primordial form of the family is the Blessed Trinity: the Father, the Son and the Holy Spirit: "The 'communion' of persons is drawn in a certain sense from the mystery of the Trinitarian

'We,' and therefore 'conjugal communion' [that is, marriage] also refers to this mystery. The family, which originates in the love of man and woman, ultimately derives from the mystery of God. This conforms to the innermost being of man and woman, to their innate and authentic dignity as persons."[1]

Earlier in the same letter, Pope John Paul II said: "In the light of the New Testament it is possible to discern how *the primordial model of the family is to be sought in God himself*, in the Trinitarian mystery of his life. The divine 'We' is the eternal pattern of the human 'we,' especially of that 'we' formed by the man and the woman created in the divine image and likeness."[2]

A good friend of mine found Pope John Paul II's words baffling. He remarked to me, "There he goes again—examining the obscure in the light of the impenetrable."

But I think my friend is wrong here. For the Trinity is not an impenetrable mystery. It's an unfathomable mystery, yes, but not impenetrable.

We can grow in our knowledge of the mystery of God, and surely he wants us to know him better. I compare it to my knowledge of my wife, Terri, whom I have known for almost a quarter-century but come to know more each day. The more I come to know her, the more I realize *how much there is to know* about her. And the more I realize that, this side of heaven, I will never have her completely figured out. As my children grow, I find them to be similarly mysterious.

As this is manifestly true of the persons I live with, so it is infinitely true of the three Persons of the Trinity. We'll never exhaust the mystery of God. We'll never be able to say we've got him completely figured out. But God does want us to grow daily in our knowledge of him.

That's why he became man, so that we would not remain in darkness about his life. The life of Christ is an ongoing revelation in time of the Trinity's inner life in eternity. Jesus revealed the Trinity not only when he spoke of the Father and the Holy Spirit but also with every action of his earthly life.

What then is the life of the Trinity? I like the way my friend Scott Hahn explains it: From all eternity God the Father pours himself out in love for the Son. He holds nothing back. The Son returns that love to the Father with everything he has. He holds nothing back. And the love that they share is the Holy Spirit. The Persons of the Trinity are life-giving lovers who give themselves completely, eternally, in all simplicity (see *CCC*, 238-267).

The Life of Love

This is also how Jesus lived his life on earth. At every moment he poured himself out in complete self-giving, in a single sacrifice that was consummated in his suffering, death and resurrection. Perhaps we have a tendency to think of Jesus' death as the moment he made his offering to God, but the Son of God made his offering from all eternity, and it was always complete—a total gift of himself, with nothing held back. The *Catechism* tells us: "The obedience of Christ in the daily routine of his hidden life was already inaugurating his work of restoring what the disobedience of Adam had destroyed" (*CCC*, 532).

In the life of the Holy Family, Joseph and Mary assisted at the daily offering of Jesus. They shared in the total offering of Jesus for the life of the world, for the sake of you and me.

This was a quiet offering, a hidden life. Yet each moment, unremembered by history, was packed with redemptive power. Some theologians say that *any* of the smallest actions of Jesus Christ—as a child at play, as a carpenter at work—would have been sufficiently powerful to redeem the world.

What was the cross but Jesus' complete outpouring of his life, the gift of himself in love, the perfect manifestation of the inner life of the Blessed Trinity in heaven and the perfect culmination of his family life on earth? I maintain that this was not something Jesus had to work up to. This was something he did every day from his infancy onward—and not by turning his erstwhile friends into goats or zapping his math teacher but by offering himself at every moment for the sake of others.

This life of self-giving, this life given for the sake of others—in heaven it's the Trinity. On earth we share in that life and love and call it *charity*. This is the love John speaks of when he says that "God is love" (1 John 4:8).

And there's much wisdom in the old saying "Charity begins at home." The life of self-giving love is the essence of the earthly family, which receives its very identity from the eternal Father, Son and Holy Spirit.

We share in the nature of God when we struggle to make our homes happy homes, when we make sacrifices for the good of others, even *and perhaps especially* when the others really get on our nerves. After all, the kernel of truth in those crazy stories about Jesus' childhood is that his friends were sometimes cruel and his teachers sometimes obtuse and egotistical. There were times, perhaps, when they deserved to have their hands withered.

The essence of family life, then, is the life of the Trinity: life that gives itself completely in love. We are baptized into Christ, and in Christ our actions, too, become redemptive. By our ordinary lives, poured out in love in imitation of the Trinity, we can redeem the world.

Bringing It All Home

How do we imitate his divine life? How do we live it day to day?

We do it the way Jesus did on earth: through daily sacrifices that culminate in a supreme sacrifice. Our homes present many opportunities for renouncing our own comfort, convenience and preferences for the good of others. Our own moral struggles challenge us to do this constantly.

When we sacrifice our desire to listen to gossip, we live the holiness of the Trinity. When we complete our daily work well for the sake of others, we live the holiness of the Trinity. When we suppress the desire to serve our children with an eviction notice and show them affection instead, we live the holiness of the Trinity.

When we do our work well and on time because our coworkers are depending on us and our family depends on our paycheck, we live the holiness of the Trinity. When we spend twenty minutes in prayer rather than watching TV or taking a nap, we live the holiness of the Trinity.

All these sacrifices are, like the cross of Christ, icons of the divine nature planted in the most ordinary and mundane corners of the life of the world.

What does it look like in the day-to-day? It looks like a mother staying up all night with a sick child or a grandmother up late with the child so that her daughter can get some sleep. It looks like a husband working overtime at a job he doesn't particularly enjoy, so that his family can know a better life. It looks like a family keeping vigil by a deathbed. It looks like the dying man who musters a smile for the sake of his loved ones.

By our everyday lives, poured out in love, we can redeem the world, beginning with our homes. We can come to see the most ordinary things as nothing less than the self-giving we are called to live in imitation of Jesus Christ, in imitation of the Holy Family, in imitation of the Trinity. For this is why God entered history by way of the family.

Here are a few practical suggestions for living this life. These are things I've learned from my parents, from my wife, from my friends and from the school of hard knocks.

1. Keep an image of the Holy Family in your home—and not just at Christmastime. This may seem like a small thing, but it goes a long way toward making the home Christ-centered. The family photos we keep on our walls are reminders of who we are, where we've come from and the standard we have to live up to.

   Back in 1890 Pope Leo XIII urged everyone to keep an image of the Holy Family on prominent display. If we don't do this, the "family" images that come into our homes will be somewhat less than holy. Think for a moment about the television families we've gawked at over the last generation or so—the Bunkers, the Simpsons, the Osbornes and the families of *Desperate Housewives*. These are, one and all, portraits of family dysfunction. But we were created for something better than that. The Holy Family is an effective antidote to family dysfunction.

2. Cultivate silence. This is the quality of the Holy Family that Pope Paul VI found especially inspiring. The Holy

Family lived a hidden life, a quiet life, a life with lots of room for thinking. I fear that with TV, radio and the Internet clogging our minds and senses we are leaving our families little room for thinking and praying. Advertising jingles crowd out our interior dialogue with God.

We should do what it takes to bring silence into our homes. One of the big changes Terri and I made many years ago was to move our TV so that it wasn't the centerpiece of the household. Now relegated to an upstairs corner, it's not on often, and it's never on when no one's watching. Try this little shift of furniture for yourself. You'll be surprised at what it'll do to lower your stress level and up your prayer life.

3. Make your home a haven of charity. One of the most striking descriptions of the early church comes from a North African writer named Tertullian. He said that it is our care of the helpless, our practice of loving kindness, that "brands" us in the eyes of others, who say, "See how they love one another."[3]

This love, this charity, has to begin at home, which Catholic tradition has called the "domestic church." Yet how many Catholics who decry the lack of reverence in their parish church then go home to desecrate their domestic churches by harsh words toward their children or their spouse or by gossip about their neighbors, their coworkers or their parish priests? Remember the words of Tertullian. They'll know we are Christians not just by the icons on our walls or the grottoes in our front yards but by the love in our hearts, expressed in our homes.

One of the great fathers of the Western church, Saint Jerome, said: "The eyes of all are turned upon you. Your house is set on a watchtower; your life fixes for others the limits of their self-control."[4]

4. Make your home a place of prayer. This doesn't mean that our days have to be dominated by devotions, but we should have some regular, routine *family* disciplines of prayer, just as the Holy Family did. They prayed and studied the Scriptures but still managed to get their work done, and so can we.

There are many ways to pray as a family, and you should seek out the ways that work best for your tribe. You can pray together at the beginning of the day or at the end of the day. You should at least offer grace at every meal. You can pray the rosary together once a week as a family. You can begin a weekly family Bible study. You can go to daily Mass.

Some friends of mine had trouble gathering their scattered children for prayer, so they started saying just one decade of the rosary together at the end of dinner. No one got up till the decade was done. It provided a nice transition from the workday to the leisurely evening.

The important thing is for us to do something, to start somewhere. We should begin with something small and manageable and then give ourselves time to grow into it. Then get ready for surprises.

Kids don't like change, and this applies to their prayer lives too. When Pope John Paul II introduced new mysteries of the rosary, Terri and I took them in stride, but our kids eyed us suspiciously the first time we said them aloud, as if we were introducing some bizarre innovation. By the time we got around to announcing the third Luminous Mystery, the wedding feast at Cana, our Gracie couldn't stand it any longer. She blurted out: "The wedding feast at K-Mart?!"

And why not? Heaven has come down to earth. It touches down in our living rooms and bedrooms and kitchens, which are holy ground, graced by our sacrament of marriage. The marriage supper of the Lamb is a permanent feast, since Jesus took the church for his bride (see Revelation 21—22). And the marriage feast is a movable feast. It goes with us wherever we drive our minivan, even to K-Mart.

God entered history by way of the family so that, by our ordinary lives poured out in love, we can coredeem the world, beginning with the place we call home.

Notes

Foreword

1. See Saint Augustine, *Confessions,* book 1, chapter 6.

Acknowledgments

1. Josemaría Escrivá, *Christ Is Passing By: Homilies* (Princeton, N.Y.: Scepter, 1974), p. 55.

Introduction: Love Amid the Frostbite

1. Pope John Paul II, *Familiaris Consortio,* Apostolic Exhortation on the Role of the Christian Family in the Modern World, November 22, 1981, no. 17, www.vatican.va.

Three: It's Verse Than I Imagined

1. Excerpt from Gerard Manley Hopkins, "Spring and Fall: To a Young Child," in *The Poems of Gerard Manley Hopkins,* 4th ed., W.H. Gardner and N.H. MacKenzie, eds. (New York: Oxford University Press, 1948), p. 89.

Four: Pilgrim's Progress

1. Oscar Wilde, *De Profundis,* www.upword.com.

Five: Bread of Laugh

1. *Luther's Small Catechism,* General Synod Edition, Part V (Philadelphia: United Lutheran Publication, 1926), p. 14.

2. Third Plenary Council of Baltimore, *A Catechism of Christian Doctrine,* Question 884 (New York: Benziger, 1921), p. 188.

Six: Mama Said

1. Herbert Ratner, *The Natural Institution of the Family* (Oak Park, Ill.: CF Reprints, 1988), pp. 9, 10.

2. Mike Aquilina, "The Priesthood of Motherhood," *Our Sunday Visitor,* May 12, 1996, p. 10.

3. Saint Augustine, Sermon 69, no. 2, *Patrologia Latina* J.P. Migne, ed., (Paris: Migne, 1841-1855), pp. 38, 441.

Seven: A Universal Call to Party

1. Pope John Paul II, "Celebrate the Day of Your Baptism!" Angelus message given January 12, 1997, no. 3, www.ewtn.com

2. Pope John Paul II, *Tertio Millennio Adveniente,* Apostolic Letter on Preparation for the Jubilee of the Year 2000, November 10, 1994, no. 41, www.vatican.va.

3. "Celebrate the Day of Your Baptism!" no. 3.

Ten: Your Priesthood

1. Pope John Paul II, *Christifideles Laici,* Apostolic Exhortation on the Vocation and the Mission of the Lay Faithful in the Church and in the World, December 30, 1988, no. 14, www.vatican.va.

2. *Christifideles Laici,* no. 14, quoting Vatican Council II, *Lumen Gentium,* Dogmatic Constitution on the Church, no. 34, www.vatican.va.

3. Vatican Council II, *Lumen Gentium,* Dogmatic Constitution on the Church, no. 34, in Walter Abbott, trans., *The Documents of Vatican II* (New York: Guild, 1966), p. 60.

Fifteen: Felines, Phobias and Faults

1. Blaise Pascal, *Pensées* (New York: E.P. Dutton, 1958), p. 78.

Seventeen: It's All I Do

1. Saint John of the Cross, "The Spiritual Canticle," John Frederick Nims, trans., *The Poems of St. John of the Cross* (New York: Grove, 1959), p. 109.

Eighteen: Dadolatry

1. Saint Thérèse of the Child Jesus, *Story of a Soul,* Thomas Taylor, ed. (London: Burnes, Oates and Washbourne, 1922), p. 79.

2. Saint Thérèse of the Child Jesus, *Story of a Soul,* John Beevers, trans. (Garden City, N.Y.: Doubleday, 1957), p. 89.

Twenty-nine: In the Public Square

1. Pamela Brennan, "Courage to Decide," *Lewisburg Daily Journal,* Lewisburg, Pa., October 14, 1994.

Thirty-four: Telling Beads

1. Quoting Vatican Council II, *Lumen Gentium,* 16.

Thirty-six: A Letter on Birth Control

1. G.K. Chesterton, *Orthodoxy* (New York: Doubleday, 1959), pp. 47–48.

Thirty-nine: The Spousal Secret

1. "God (or Not), Physics and, of Course, Love: Scientists Take a Leap," *New York Times,* January 4, 2005, section F, page 3.

Forty: By Way of the Family

1. Pope John Paul II, Letter to Families, February 2, 1994, no. 8, www.vatican.va.

2. Letter to Families, no. 6.

3. Tertullian, *Apology,* chapter 39, *Ante-Nicene Fathers: Translations of the Writings of the Fathers Down to A.D. 325,* vol. 3, Alexander Roberts and James Donaldson, eds. (New York: Charles Scribner's Sons, 1926), p. 46.

4. Saint Jerome, Letter 60, no. 14, *A Select Library of the Christian Church: Nicene and Post-Nicene Fathers,* vol. 6, *Jerome: Letters and Select Works,* second series Philip Schaff and Henry Wace, eds. (Peabody, Mass.: Hendrickson, 2004), p. 129.

CPSIA information can be obtained at www.ICGtesting.com
Printed in the USA
BVOW06s1644250815

414962BV00007B/21/P